Charles E. Vredenburgh

The Case Against the Church

Charles E. Vredenburgh

The Case Against the Church

ISBN/EAN: 9783337331740

Printed in Europe, USA, Canada, Australia, Japan

Cover: Foto ©Lupo / pixelio.de

More available books at **www.hansebooks.com**

THE
CASE AGAINST THE CHURCH.

THE following passage, containing the essence of pure materialism, is, singularly enough, seldom commented on by the clergy:

"I said in my heart concerning **the** estate of the sons of men, that God might manifest them, and that they might see that they themselves are beasts. For that which befalleth the sons of men befalleth beasts; even one thing befalleth them: as the one dieth, so dieth the other; yea, they have all one breath; so that a man hath no pre-eminence above a beast: for all is vanity. All go unto one place; all are of the dust, and all turn to dust again. Who knoweth the spirit of man that goeth upward [In the Septuagint, "If it goeth upward"], and the spirit of the beast that goeth downward to the earth? Wherefore I perceive that there is nothing better than that a man should rejoice in his own works; for that is his portion: for who shall bring him to see what shall be after him?—ECCLESIASTES III, 18-22.

THE
Case Against the Church

A SUMMARY OF THE ARGUMENTS
AGAINST CHRISTIANITY.

"Not giving heed to Jewish fables."—TITUS I, 14.

NEW YORK:
CHARLES P. SOMERBY,
139 Eighth Street.
1876.

Copyrighted.
1876.

C. P. SOMERBY,
Printer and Electrotyper,
139 Eighth Street, New York.

PREFATORY NOTE.

The object of this essay is to present in outline the arguments against Christianity from the standpoint of materialism. These arguments have never, so far as I am aware, been collected together in a condensed form. The word skeptic implies, to the average church-member, the idea of a monster of wickedness, destitute of all moral restraint, capable of committing any crime in the calendar, and who always recants his opinions upon his death-bed. The clergy are at no pains to correct these erroneous impressions, and set clearly before the laity the points in dispute between the Church and her opponents. Indeed, it is not to their interest to do so. I have, therefore, thought that an attempt to sum up the case on the part of science, would not be amiss at this time, when the matter is attracting such general attention. Of course, in treating a subject of such magnitude in so limited a space, anything like attention to detail is impossible. For the latter, the reader is referred to the literature of the discussion. This question cannot be set at rest by abusing scientific men, or by falling back upon *a priori* assumptions and appeals to the emotions. It must be *argued*, and the victory awaits that party which shall produce the most conclusive evidence.

THE
CASE AGAINST THE CHURCH.

It is part of the nature of a reasonable being to inquire the causes of the various phenomena, subjective and objective, in the midst of which he has his existence. There are two ways by which such a being attempts to solve the question, "Whence the origin and maintenance of nature, animate and inanimate?" These are, on the one hand, the appeal to "inner consciousness," and, on the other, observation and induction. Upon the former are based all religious systems; upon the latter, all science. The former is the first to occur to man in the savage condition, who transfers his moods and passions to external nature, and sees in her phenomena the actions of a being like himself, only much larger. The latter method of thought does not arise until at a later stage in man's intellectual development; and, being in all its workings the exact opposite of its predecessor, the struggle between the two for the mastery is hot and bitter, always resulting, however, in victory for the exact method.

The appeal to consciousness, not resting upon any fixed basis, but being guided only by the emotions, we have, as a natural result, many different forms of religion.

Facts, on the other hand, being " stubborn things," there can be only one science, using the word in its broadest sense.

Long after the importance and **utility of the scientific method are** recognized, the emotional mode **of thought retains its** sway, though much restricted as to territory. **An** inherited tendency to superstition cannot be eradicated in one or two generations, and it is to this superstitious predilection that religion appeals with tremendous power. Men (and more especially women) like to believe in the mysterious and supernatural. **But** against the phantasies of superstition, the calm deductions of exact science are like a broadside of artillery directed at the frailest glass. To paraphrase an old proverb, When science enters at the door, superstition flies out at the window. Obviously, the remedy is, to keep science from entering at the door, and this is the policy actually pursued. "The great things of religion," say its votaries, "are beyond the scope of science." Nothing that man can think about is beyond the scope of science. And what is theology but an attempt to form a science, albeit by unscientific methods, out of these very subjects?

Of the various forms of religion, we are here concerned with but one—Christianity. Originating in Palestine, this faith possessed no particular power until it assumed a political policy, and allied itself with the Roman Empire. Pure as are many of its teachings, its success is to be attributed rather to force than to the high tone of its morality—to the fire at the stake, **rather** than to that of the cloven tongues. Of course, **there** is mixed up with the ethics of Christianity the **usual** amount of absurd mythology which we find in all religions. It follows that between the believers in this latter and students of nature there is an intellectual war, not always conducted in the most amiable manner by the Church. Science has no object but the establishment of the truth, while the Church stands committed to the defense of her system, down to the minutest details, even after it is demonstrated to be false. This fact gives to science decidedly the advantage. It is my purpose here to recapitulate briefly the arguments against the Christian religion, or rather against the Christian mythology, in order to define clearly the motives of scientists for rejecting it as incompatible with reason.

What, then, is Christianity? What are its claims upon our belief? How are those claims sustained?

It speaks to us with authority, to begin with. It asserts that it was delivered unto man by God himself. With such an origin it should stand the most searching investigation. It further declares that God is one, yet composed of three persons—Father, Son, and Holy Ghost. That God created the universe in five days (indefinite periods?), the creation of man occupying the sixth. That God thereupon rested the seventh day, and has been ever since quiescent, so far as acts of creation are concerned. That God placed man in a paradise (a Persian term signifying a pleasure-garden), and afterward made woman from one of his ribs. That man was created pure, enlightened, and holy, but fell from that condition to one of sin and suffering. (Christianity does not insist very strongly upon the literal acceptance of the story of the manner in which he fell.) That labor and death were entailed upon him as a punishment for his disobedience, the earth having previously brought forth its fruits without cultivation, and man himself having been immortal. That the immediate descendants of the first man attained to great age, from six to nine centuries not being at all uncommon. That God the Father, to demonstrate his own power and **glory**, promised to send God the Son upon earth to assume a human form, suffer, and die; by his death restoring man to the condition from which he fell. That, on account of the wickedness of mankind, God destroyed them **all**, with the exception of one family, by a deluge which covered the tops of the highest mountains, and, after remaining forty days, was dried up by a wind. That the family above mentioned, who were saved in an ark, repeopled the earth, one of the three sons populating Europe, another Asia, and the third Africa. Draper pertinently observes that as the existence of America was not known at that time, no ancestor was provided for it. We are further told that the rainbow was set in the heavens as a sign that the flood should never happen again. That the postdiluvian race, for some unexplained reason, attempted to build a tower as high as heaven, which God resenting, confounded their language; this being the reason that all mankind do not speak the same tongue. That God particularly favored the descendants of a man named Jacob, and delivered to them his will. That it was to them his Son was to appear. That unto them, accordingly, the Son did come, assuming the form of Jesus of Nazareth. That Jesus was born of the Virgin Mary, but of no earthly father. That during his life, he worked many miracles, as an evidence of his divinity. That having been put to death by the Roman authority, he rose from the dead, and ascended visibly into heaven. That by his death he delivered mankind from the consequences of the Fall.

That there is a state of rewards and punishments after death for those who accept or refuse the atonement. **That** after the ascension of Jesus, the Holy Ghost came to earth, and rested upon the apostles in the shape of tongues of fire, the apostles being thus enabled to speak all languages without having learned them. That the world will finally be destroyed by fire. Previous to this, however, all the dead will be raised, and Jesus will reappear in the clouds of heaven, and in his proper character of God the Son. That a state of happiness for the righteous, and of misery for the wicked, will then ensue, to endure forever, the apportionment to which will take place at a general judgment to occur after the resurrection.

Such, in brief, are the prominent points of Christianity; those upon which all sects, with one or two exceptions, are agreed. If we attempt to define the system much more closely, we strike upon points of difference among Christians themselves, which increase so rapidly that we are bewildered, and inclined to think that Christianity, instead of being one religion, is at least a score. The majority of Christians, however. hold the positions I have enumerated. It is for me, therefore, to consider these in detail, and determine whether any or all are sufficiently sustained by evidence to command the belief of an intelligent, unprejudiced thinker.

As to its claim to divine origin, all religions have made the same assertion. In fact, a religion which was confessedly the invention of man would have very few followers, and would be of extremely short duration. In passing judgment upon this claim, we must be guided by our results in regard to the system itself. If we find its assertions borne out by proof, that will be evidence in favor of its divine origin. If we are able **to disprove** those assertions—nay, if we can overthrow a single one—we must either make God a liar, or admit that the origin of Christianity is human.

As to the nature of God, the Jews were monotheists. No such doctrine as that of the Trinity was known to them. Nor was it taught in the Christian Church till it was brought prominently forward by the See of Alexandria. The idea of a trinity was perfectly familiar to the Egyptians, as forming part of their ancient mythology, but had previously found no place in the Christian scheme. For our definition of the doctrine, let us resort to the Westminster Catechism. That compendium of Christian faith tells us that " there are three persons in the Godhead: the Father, Son, and Holy Ghost; and these three are one God—the same in substance, equal in power and glory."

This dogma is, in the first place, extremely illogical. If the word person means anything at all, it implies **dis**tinct individuality. Three persons must be three individuals. To say that these three persons are one person, and insist upon this as an article of belief, is to affront common sense. The endeavors which have been made to reconcile it with reason are peculiarly lame. A favorite illustration is that of three candles, or sources of light. As three candles, it is said, give but one light, so the three persons of the Trinity, though indistinct, are one God. This is not exactly a parallel statement. To make it so, it should be asserted that the three candles are one candle. Taking it as it stands, however, its premises are false. Three candles **do not give** one light, but three lights. Each casts **a shadow as if** the others were absent, as may easily **be proved by** trying the experiment. Each maintains a separate and distinct individuality. The fate of **this illustration** awaits all others. It is impossible to demonstrate that three **are one.**

In the second place, this doctrine, which occupies such a prominent place in the majority of Christian sects, is entirely rejected by others. When it was first pro**posed,** it met with bitter opposition from Arius of Alex**andria.** That prelate took the ground that the Son had not always existed, "since it is a necessary condition of the filial relation that a father should be older than his son."* Though its author was excommunicated and anathematized, the Arian heresy spread and gained many supporters. In our own day, the dogma of the Trinity is denied by the Unitarians. This sect, however, is called unorthodox. If the Unitarians could succeed in gaining **a** majority in the Church, the negative particle would quickly disappear from that adjective.

Accordingly we find that Christianity, while asserting **that** it worships but one God, in reality worships three. Christians pray to God the Father, closing their petitions with "for the sake of thy Son." They also implore him to "send his Holy Spirit" upon earth. He is moreover spoken of as having "sent" his Son to suffer and die. A separate individuality is thus plainly implied, if not openly confessed. If the Father and Son are the same in substance, why pray to the one, appealing to his love for the other? If they are equal in power, **why** not pray directly to the Son? **If** the presence of the Holy Ghost be desired, why not address the **request to that person of** the Godhead? Yet prayer is

---

* Draper's "Conflict of Religion and Science," p. 53.

always made to the Father, to whom, throughout the entire utterances of the Church, a prominence is ascribed which is not awarded to the other members of the Trinity. He is the chief person in **the divine trio**. The very expressions I have quoted in reference to the Father's "sending" the Son or the Spirit, and the common phrases, "mission of the Son," "mission of the Spirit," imply an act of command on the part of the Father, and of obedience on that of the other persons of the Trinity, which carries with it the idea of the superiority of the former. A Christian would be shocked at the mention of the Son's "sending" the Father upon any mission. God the Father is never spoken of as having died upon the cross. Yet if the three persons of the Godhead be the same, and *one* God, it certainly would seem as if one of them could not perform any act not shared in equally by the others.

Thus the Church, while accepting the dogma in name, repudiates it in fact. It is a mere form of words, for no mind ever was, or ever will be, formed, that can grasp the idea. It is unthinkable.

Its divine origin falls to the ground when we follow out its history, for we can trace it to its starting-point in the second century. The Apostles' creed, probably the oldest confession of Christian faith extant, says, "I believe **in** God the Father Almighty . . . and in Jesus Christ His only Son, our Lord. . . . **I** believe in the Holy Ghost." Nowhere does it express or imply that "these three are one God." The human authorship of the doctrine is beyond all question.

Before touching upon the statements of the Church regarding the creation and governance of the world, it **is well** that we pause to examine the authority supported by which she takes her position. That authority is the Bible. What, then, is the Bible? Turning to the work itself for our answer, we find it to be a collection of sixty-six books by different authors and on various subjects. Some of the books are historical, others poetical, while others again are collections of moral aphorisms and discourses upon religious subjects. The Church claims for these sixty-six books divine origin, and asserts that they contain the sum of all truth, physical as well as moral. But the books themselves admit that they were written by men, each one bearing the name of its real or reputed author. The form, therefore, in which the Church asserts their divinity is that of inspiration. Exactly what inspiration means, I have never found any one who could tell. The nearest approach to a definition, is the declaration that the authors of the Bible wrote under the direction of God. It is an explanation which in reality explains nothing, but only repeats the difficulty in other words. Were these men merely machines, writing from an invisible dictation? If so, how was this dictation given? And if it was so subtle that this question cannot be answered, what proof have we that it existed at all? Here the Church meets us with an answer—her great, and, indeed, only reply to our last inquiry—Internal Evidence. The work, she asserts, is its own proof. In order that this ground may be maintained, the Bible should contain nothing that can be disproved. It is the object of our present **investigation** to learn if this be so.

There is one point in reference to the Bible which must forcibly strike every one who considers the subject. It is, Why do these sixty-six books, written in different ages by men of different habits of mind, and in different languages—exactly these and no other—constitute the Bible? What man or set of men, possessed the discretionary ability to accept certain books as divinely inspired, and reject others as of purely human authorship? And when was this assembling of the Bible done? If at the beginning of the Christian era, why has the Bible in all subsequent ages not been the same? Yet the Septuagint version, which was used exclusively in Egypt and the East, contains a number of books not now recognized as canonical. In regard to even those which are common to all editions, manuscripts **differ.** The Codex Vaticanus, the basis of our later versions, contains extensive passages not found in the Codex Sinaiticus, admitted to be an older manuscript. It was not until the Councils of Nice, Laodicea, and, further on, that of Trent, that any authoritative utterance proceeded from the Church relative to the Bible. **The latter** Council completed what the two former ones had begun. The several books were admitted to the Bible by the **vote** of the majority. It is said that the Gospel of Luke was carried by one vote. The case, therefore, stands thus: God inspired various men to write the books of the Bible, but left it to a purely human **assemblage to** determine, centuries later, which books were the product **of such** inspiration, and which were not. Two passing thoughts suggest themselves here: First, **God** seems to have cared very little about the Bible himself, or he would have taken better care of it. Secondly, if the councils spoken of had voted differently, which they were just as likely to do, the sacred canon would not be the same as we have it at present: now, is there not a **possi**bility that mistakes were made—what should have **been rejected** being admitted, and *vice versa?* The only means of escaping this dilemma is the belief in the infallibility of the Church. Catholics who accept this dogma have already sacrificed their reason, **and are not** amenable to argument; Protestants, who **reject it, must** admit the force of the objection.

Upon the basis of the Bible, the Church has constructed a scheme of cosmogony, the only drawback to which is its utter absurdity. One by one her positions, in regard to physical science have been assailed, and one by one they have been carried. In not a single instance can she point to a victory. To begin at the beginning, let us take the subject of the creation of the world and its inhabitants. As representing the views of the extremists in the Church, I quote from a work entitled " The Foundations of **History," by Samuel B. Shieffelin** (1865). The author is a specimen of a somewhat *rara avis* at this time—a man who openly, and in print, maintains the literal accuracy of the Mosaic record. Others have endeavored to establish harmony between that narrative and certain well-ascertained facts. No such temporizing measures will suit Mr. Shieffelin. With a lordly supremacy, he waves the facts of science to one side, and takes his stand by the record, *verbatim et literatim*.

On page 21, after stating that the age of the earth can be determined only by adding together the ages of the Hebrew patriarchs, Mr. Shieffelin finally settles the date of creation at 4004 B.C. He then proceeds to state that, **"In the** account of creation we are told very plainly that ' in **six days God** created the heavens and the earth ': **not indefinite eras, or periods** of time, but evenings and mornings, days. For wise reasons the **Creator** took that time; instead of speaking all things into being in one instant, which he could as easily have done. . . . Let us remember this that we may 'avoid the oppositions of science,* falsely so called.' We must also remember that everything when created was immediately complete in itself; trees, animals and man, each when made were full grown, full size and perfect. Each also having the wonderful faculty of perpetuating its species." Mr. Shieffelin adds, by way of reflection upon the above, " No wonder that at the completion of such a work, 'the sons of God shouted for joy!'" Truly, it would have been no wonder had they shouted somewhat for astonishment as well.

Upon the other hand, what says science about the creation of the world? That it never was created at all. Science teaches us that there are in space vast masses of nebulous matter in a gaseous state. The telescope reveals to us these objects, and that wonderful instrument, the spectroscope, unfolds to us their constitution. Given such a mass, its particles endowed with mutual attraction and repulsion, and what will be the result? It will begin to rotate, as the nebula in Canes Venatici has already commenced to do. As the rotation becomes faster and faster, and the mass assumes a spheroidal form, centrifugal force begins to assert its sway. A ring will be thrown off from the whirling nebula. As the centrifugal force enlarges that ring more and more, it finally becomes unable to retain its form. A break occurs at the weakest part, its particles collect themselves together, and we have a planet revolving about the central mass. All this while the nebula has been losing heat. Its atoms are approaching each other more

---

* The word $\gamma\nu\tilde{\omega}\sigma\iota\varsigma$ in II Tim. vi, 20, does not mean science, as we now use the term, but knowledge generally.

closely, and the mass becomes denser and denser. A second ring is thrown off, and another planet is the result. After a time the central mass has cooled until it is much more compact than at first. The rings which it then throws off are smaller, friction of the particles and diminished momentum preventing the disengagement of as large masses as formerly. The interior planets are therefore smaller than the exterior. At length the central mass becomes so dense that it will throw off rings no longer. It remains, therefore, a sun surrounded by a family of planets. These latter bodies, however, have not been idle all this time. They have been imitating the nebula from which they sprang, throwing off rings which become satellites. The outer planets, being the larger, and their density being less than that of the inner, will have the greatest number of these attendants. In this way, science asserts that the solar system was formed. But is not this creation? Not at all. Creation implies an act, while in this whole process there is nothing sudden; the condition of the nebulous mass at any moment being the direct resultant of its condition at the previous moment, and not of any arbitrary fiat. Moreover, we are led to believe that the system will again be resolved into nebula, to undergo anew the process of condensation, as it has been undergone no one can say how often already. Science teaches us that this rhythmic ebb and flow is infinite, and leads us with irresistible force to the grand conclusion—the eternity of matter.

So much for the statements on both sides; now for the proofs. What evidence has the Church to offer in support of her theory? Nothing but the bare assertion of Genesis—a narrative which bears upon its face the marks of its legendary character. A narrative, moreover, whose accuracy and very authenticity have been disproved beyond question by learned men in the Church herself. The discussion on the subject of the Pentateuch may be found, in a condensed form, in Draper's "Conflict of Religion and Science," page 220. It is sufficient here to mention among those who have denied its authenticity the names of St. Jerome, Clement of Alexandria, Irenæus, Hengstenberg, and Colenso. Hupfeld sums up the matter thus: "The discovery that the Pentateuch is put together out of various sources, or original documents, is beyond all doubt not only one of the most important and most pregnant with consequences for the interpretation of the historical books of the Old Testament, or rather for the whole of theology and history, but it is also one of the most certain discoveries which have been made in the domain of criticism and the history of literature. Whatever the anticritical party may bring forward to the contrary, it will maintain itself, and not retrograde again through anything, so long as there exists such a thing as criticism; and it will not be easy for a reader upon the stage of culture on which we stand in the present day, if he goes to the examination unprejudiced, and with an uncorrupted power of appreciating the truth, to be able to ward off its influence."* Apart from mere unbacked assertion, is there a single fact in nature which tends to prove the Mosaic account of the creation? Not one.

On the other hand, what has science to offer in support of the nebular theory? The reasons for receiving it are numerous and convincing. They are:

---

* Draper. Op. cit. p. 224.

I. The existence of nebulæ in different quarters of the heavens, in various stages of condensation and rotation. From the great nebula of Orion to the rings of Saturn, we have all the most important steps of the process before our eyes; and the inference is so plain that "he who runs may read." The nebular theory is written in flaming characters upon the very vault of heaven.

II. The orbits of the planets and satellites are ellipses of so slight eccentricity that they are practically circular.

III. All the motions (with one exception) are from west to east. This holds good of the rotation of planets and satellites upon their axes, of the revolution of satellites about their primaries, and of the course of the latter around the sun. It is impossible that so many coincidences should be the result of chance. Let us hear Mr. Proctor upon this subject. In his last lecture in New York (1873), he said: "The actual probabilities are great against anything like chance distribution of the Solar System, particularly when we remember that there are 142 primary and secondary planets, and when we take into account their motion alone, each circling around the sun in the same direction. The chance that one is going in one direction, and the next going in the same direction, is only one chance out of two; and the chance that a third would go in the same direction is only one chance out of four; the chance that a fourth would go likewise is only one out of eight; a fifth, one out of sixteen. So we must go on doubling until we find that the chance of 142 planets going round in the same direction—I hope you will be patient while I tell you the number—is one in 2,774,800,000,000,000 000,000,000,000,000,000,000,000!" Truly, a fearful odds. We are led irresistibly, therefore, to the conclusion that the Solar System, as it exists to-day, is the result of law. But law is inconsistent and irreconcilable with arbitrary, sovereign, personal action.

IV. The exterior planets are larger than the interior, and have more satellites.

V. The explanation of the rings of Saturn is obvious, and is possible upon no other supposition.

VI. We find the sun composed of materials similar to those of which the earth consists, which is evidence in favor of their having been originally one body.

VII. The larger planets rotate more rapidly than the smaller ones.

VIII. The oblateness of the earth and other planets shows that they were once in a soft and plastic condition.

Upon these facts the nebular theory is grounded. Opposed to it we have—what? A mere legend—a phantom. Certainly the strongest case is that of science.

But how about life, vegetable and animal? Shall we hold that the immense worlds which unceasingly roll about the sun became what they are through the operation of law, and yet be forced to accept the theory of creation to explain the existence of living things? Let us see about this. Upon the one hand we have the statement of the Church, which for convenience I have allowed Mr. Shieffelin to represent, to the effect that "everything when created was immediately complete in itself; trees, animals, and man, each when made were full grown, full size, and perfect."

Upon the other hand, we have the statement of science that the same laws which formed the Solar System and the Universe, gave rise to all life, animal and vegetable. To get at the root of this matter we must commence very far back. Dissolve sal-ammoniac, or any other salt, in water, and spread some of the solution upon a glass plate. As the water evaporates, the salt finally becomes unable to retain the liquid form. Its molecules approach one another, drawn by the same power which set the chaotic nebula in revolution, and an exhibition of polar force takes place truly wonderful to the thoughtful mind. A tiny dot makes its appearance upon the glass, from which presently shoots forth a thin, delicate, needle-like crystal. Another and another such crystal grows like magic under the eye, until the entire surface is covered with fern-like forms of exquisite beauty. Whence this structural power? Was it by direct intervention of Almighty God, or in consequence of forces inherent in the salt? No one, not even a Christian, would hesitate in his reply to this question. Every one would answer that the latter was the correct explanation. Now let us take one of these crystals and examine it by means of polarized light. We notice certain chromatic phenomena. Substitute for the crystal a grain of wheat, and effects are produced not differing in kind from those in the former case. What is the unavoidable inference? That the crystal and the grain, though composed of different substances, are, since they produce like effects upon light-waves, constructed in a similar manner, and by the operation of the same agency. In the case of the crystal, we have seen that this agency is molecular force. Shall we deny it in the case of the grain?

But let us plant our grain of wheat in the earth. Surrounded, then, by materials similar to its own, and placed under conditions favorable to their appropriation, inevitable molecular force draws these substances to the grain. It sprouts, grows, and produces a living plant. To effect this, heat is necessary. Now, heat is motion among the constituent particles of a body. Once set in motion, the atoms of carbon, hydrogen, nitrogen, and oxygen, are free to obey the dictates of attractive force. Oblige them to remain at rest, and this result is impossible. Wheat has been taken from Egyptian tombs, where it had lain for centuries, and, upon being planted, has grown like the seed of last year. Was the grain living during all that time? Will the tiny embryo retain the principle of life uninjured for two thousand years, when the full grown and vigorous plant survives but one season? Or shall we not rather believe that the grain of wheat when taken from its long repose, was as lifeless as the inert crystal, and that life only resulted when it was placed under proper conditions, by the operation of purely physical force? Vegetable life would therefore seem to be a resultant of natural forces, rather than a separate and independent principle. But how is it in regard to the animal? Surely here we have complexity of organism which requires for explanation something more than mere structural energy. Let us not be misled here. Complexity is in itself no ground for asserting radical difference. Out of the same stone of which the rude cromlech is built may be constructed the magnificent cathedral, by the same agency—muscular force directed by architectural taste. Complexity in this case merely implies more extended operation of the same factors. Science holds that a similar relation exists between the vegetable and the animal. Between the oak and man there is an immense difference, discernible at once; but between the lower orders of vegetable and the lower orders of animal life the variation is so slight that it is often a point of the greatest difficulty to determine to which class a specimen belongs. **As we** lose complexity, and approach simplicity, the two orders of life approximate more and more closely. But it is **asserted** that the life of a man is vastly higher in the **scale than** that of the lower animals, and that this distance constitutes radical difference. Let us examine into this. Lower a plummet into the sea until it touches bottom. Upon drawing it up again, you will probably find sticking to it a gelatinous substance. Scrape off a a little of this, and examine it under the microscope. It will be found to be composed of separate masses of a perfectly homogeneous, albuminoid matter. These little bodies are protoplasm cells. Moreover, they are **living** animals. Destitute of organs, they nevertheless perform all the functions necessary to the prolongation of their existence. They move about without muscles, see **their** prey (*sic*) without eyes, eat without a mouth, and **digest** without an intestinal canal. When one of them travels through the water, it stretches out a portion of its jelly-like substance in front, and draws up the rear-part; repeating this again and again, the result being a slow movement, called from the name of the animal, amœboid. When it becomes aware of its prey, it stretches out two portions to serve as arms, literally puts itself outside of its food, and for the time being becomes all stomach. The nutritive portion of the food **is absorbed into** the substance of the amœba, and the useless part rejected. This latter **creature is** the simplest form of animal life. Nothing but a glutinous particle, without organization, or structure of any kind, it preserves its existence with as much apparent judgment as the most highly educated human being.

From this tiny dot to man is seemingly an immense distance. It is not really, however, as great as it appears. Man has a bony skeleton, overlaid with muscles which serve to move its various parts. But the muscles are not capable of spontaneous action. They must first be irritated, and then they contract. This is all they can do. The irritation is the result of reflex nervous action. Now, the nervous system in man (and these remarks apply to all the vertebrate animals) is composed of two different substances—a white matter and a gray matter. The white matter forms the nerve filaments, which serve to transmit impulses, but which of themselves are as inert as the muscles. The gray matter constitutes he nerve-centers—the brain, and other **ganglia**. From these the commands are issued which, carried along the white substance, finally cause the muscles to contract. Examining the gray matter, what do we find? Large numbers of little albuminous, homogeneous particles—in a word, protoplasm cells. We do not find these in the bones, the muscles, or the white substance of the nerve filaments. Let us inspect that most delicate organ of special sense, the eye. Embodied in the retina, without which the eye would be blind, we again discover these minute bodies. In a word, wherever in an animal we find a seat of self-originated impulse, there we find also cells of protoplasm similar to those we draw from the depths of the sea. When these are lacking, those portions of the body **are** inert until acted upon by this marvelous substance. **We** may go further still. If we trace man himself backward **through** intra-uterine life, we find him originate in a little albuminous, inorganized, yet self-moving particle—a protoplasm cell. Truly, protoplasm is, in the words ot another, "the common denominator of life." The life of a man is the sum of the energies of all the protoplasm cells entering into the construction of his frame. Organization is crystallization. Every physician knows that the plastic material in the interior of ovarian cysts often forms itself into jaw-bones filled with teeth, into hair, etc. Such material will as inevitably organize under proper conditions, as a solution of a salt will crystallize under like favorable circumstances. The difference between the organic and inorganic world is, like every other distinction in nature, one of degree, not of kind. There are no sharp lines drawn anywhere.

Did man, then, originate from the protoplasm cell? And if so, in what manner? Science teaches us that it was by a process analogous to that by which the Solar System arose from the nebula—a process of evolution. There were many steps between the little cell and the genus described in works of natural history as Homo Sapiens. Some of these steps are obliterated, but enough remain to point out, like scattered landmarks, the path from the past to the present. The theory of development enunciated by Darwin and Wallace, and further extended by Herbert Spencer (who applies it also to the explanation of mental phenomena), marks the greatest advance of thought for centuries. My limits are too small to give even a hasty resume of the theory. A definition of it by Professor Huxley is all I have space for. The latter says:

"Mr. Darwin's hypothesis . . . . is, that all the phenomena of organic nature, past and present, result from, or are caused by, the interaction of those properties of organic **matter** which we have called ATAVISM (Heredity) and VARIABILITY, with the CONDITIONS OF EXISTENCE; or, in other words—given the existence of organic matter, its tendency to transmit its properties, and its tendency occasionally to vary; and lastly, given the conditions of existence by which organic matter is surrounded—that these put together are the causes of the Present **and of** the Past conditions of ORGANIC NATURE."[*]

The evidence in favor of these views is manifold. We can hardly look about us without discovering fresh proof. The theory **is "encompassed** with so great a cloud of witnesses" that it is accepted by all the prominent thinkers of to-day. From such a mass of testimony I select but one point. It is the existence of rudimentary organs. We find in man and other animals **organs** which are incapable **of** being used, but which **are the** analogues of fully developed and useful organs in some lower species of beings. Man, for instance, has muscles attached to the external ear. These muscles are atrophied, and exsanguine in appearance. Man cannot move the ear with them, and no advantage would be gained if he could. Upon the creation hypothesis, what shall **we** say of these organs? That hypothesis asserts that everything was made for some wise purpose, and declared to be "very good"; yet here are parts of the body which, the advocates of creation must admit, were evidently made to **serve** no purpose whatsoever. In the apes, however, we find these muscles fully developed, and of the greatest use to the animal, enabling him **to** hear the approach of the slightest danger, and thus act-

---

[*] Lectures on the Origin of Species, p. 131.

ing as agents for his preservation. **What is** the inference? That there was a time when **man**, too, needed such a means **of** protection; when he, too, in his wild state had the power of using these now effete organs; and that although they have been transmitted from one generation to another, ages of disuse have caused them **to** dwindle into mere rudiments of what they formerly **were. Is** not this the more rational explanation? There **are** numerous other examples of the same thing—the lineæ albæ of the abdominal rectus muscle, and the caudal remnant called the coccyx, for instance. Shall we deny that all life comes from the protoplasm cell, when **it** is a fact capable of visible demonstration, that every individual living being thus originates, passing, during its embryonic life, through many of the types which science asserts the race to have undergone?

So from chaos to cosmos, from the tiny monad **up** to man, science teaches that there is an undivided chain, an unbroken series. It is like the spectrum, the extreme **colors of** which stand in vivid contrast, yet shade into each other by gradations so delicate that no one can say where one color ends and the next begins.

But a process like this requires time. Millions **of** years must elapse before any marked **change** is apparent. Untold ages must **pass** away before the whole is completed. Completed, did I **say**? Nay, it is never finished—it is a succession whose duration is infinite.

In view of these premises, how fares the assertion of the Church that God created the universe in **six** days (which word, **I agree** with Mr. Shieffelin, **does** not mean indefinite periods), making every **living** thing at once perfect? Will it **bear the** calm light of reason? I think not. Moreover, **the** existence of systems forming in space before our eyes shows that **the Sabbath of rest,** instead of having been inaugurated **six thousand years** ago, has not yet begun, and nature gives **no promise of** its commencement.

There is a more moderate party in the Church, which endeavors to reconcile Genesis with the inevitable truths above enumerated. They have undertaken a hopeless task. The two things are absolutely incompatible both in letter and spirit. If science teaches the truth, Genesis must be a fable. But science comes to us backed by the strongest, most unimpeachable evidence, while Genesis is supported by nothing. It has to face a set of charges sufficiently well established to break down the credibility of any modern work. But the Bible, says the Church, is not to be judged by the same standard as other books. That is begging the question. Its right of immunity from such criticism is exactly what the Church has failed to prove.

But if we dismiss the Mosaic narrative as a fable, it carries with it the story of the Fall. The foundation is knocked from under the doctrine of the Atonement, and the plan of salvation falls to the ground. Let us read over the account of the Fall, and see what meaning we gather **from it.** It is found in Genesis iii, and runs in this **wise:**

"**Now the** serpent was more subtile than any beast of the field **which** the Lord God had made: and he said unto the woman, **Yea,** hath God said, Ye shall not eat of every tree of the garden? And the woman said unto the serpent, We may eat of the fruit of the trees of the garden; but of the tree which is in the midst of the garden, God hath said, Ye shall not eat of it, neither shall ye touch it, lest ye die. And the serpent said unto the woman, **Ye shall not surely die: for God doth know,** that in the day ye eat **thereof, then** your eyes shall be opened; and ye shall be as gods, knowing good and evil. And when the woman saw that the tree was good for food, and that it was pleasant to the eyes, and a tree to be desired to make one wise; she took of the fruit thereof, and did eat; and gave also unto her husband with her, and he did eat. And the eyes of them both were opened, and they knew that they were naked; and they sewed fig-leaves together, and made themselves aprons." Here let us stop for a moment, and rest. If this tale formed no part of the sacred canon, but were **to** be exhumed in our own day, there is not an intelligent man living, in the Church or out, who would not set it down as a legend. Having the warrant of antiquity, however, it acquires respectability. The serpent is said to be the Devil; why, it would be difficult to state, as the narrative itself nowhere asserts or implies any such thing. Apparently the only reason for making the statement is an expression in Rev. xii, 9, in which the Evil One is spoken of as "that old serpent." If, however, we grant, for the sake of argument, that such is the case, we are involved in a worse perplexity a little further on. Let us continue our reading:

"And **they** heard the voice of the Lord God walking (!) in the garden in the cool of the day: and Adam and his wife hid themselves from the presence of **the** Lord God amongst the trees of the garden. And **the Lord** God called unto Adam, and said unto him, Where art thou?" Adam was evidently effectually hidden! . . . "**And** the Lord God said unto the serpent, Because thou hast done this, thou art cursed above all cattle, and above every beast of the field: upon thy belly shalt thou go, and dust shalt thou eat all the days of thy life." Here we encounter the difficulty referred to above. If the serpent was merely a form assumed by the Devil, why was a punishment inflicted upon the actual animal? That the reptile here spoken of is a *bona fide* serpent there can be no doubt, from the sentence pronounced upon him; which has no meaning whatever if applied to the Evil One. The passage quoted suggests an inquiry for the curious, and contains an inaccuracy. Inquiry—how did the serpent go before he went upon his belly? Inaccuracy—the serpent does not eat dust.

Such is the story which the Christian Church actually expects persons not so low in intellectual condition as the Hottentot to believe. Regardless of the degrading conception it presents, of Almighty God nearly outwitted by man, and quite outwitted by the serpent; unmindful of its inconsistencies, absurdities, and impossibilities; blind to the fact that there exists no difference in character between this legend and the legends (admitted to be such) of "gentile" nations; heedless of all these obvious truths, the Church makes this story (than which the Arabian Nights contains nothing more wild) the basis of her religious scheme, and tells us we must receive it as the word of God! After this, who shall attempt to set a limit to human credulity?

The Church, however, is logical in insisting upon the retention of this fable. It is necessary that man should have fallen, in order that the plan of salvation may have a basis upon which to rest. Science teaches us, in opposition to this, that so far from man having fallen from a higher estate, he has been steadily advancing from a lower; so that whether the story of the Fall be considered as allegory or as truthful narration, it is equally untenable. It is **impossible that any such occurrence** could ever have taken place.

In passing from **the Fall** to the Deluge, I only **stop to** notice the extraordinary length of life to which it is **asserted** that the patriarchs attained. The veracious historians seem to have thought that figures were a mere bagatelle, **so** long as they told a big story. Accordingly, **different** editions of the Bible give different ages; all, however, large. The Septuagint makes Methuselah live until after the Deluge, which inclines us pensively to reflect upon the remarkable swimming powers of the old gentleman. It is impossible to write seriously upon this subject, the only emotion which it excites being **a kind of** contemptuous wonder that any one should be found to believe a thing so utterly preposterous.

Here, again, the moderate party attempts to explain this uncommon longevity by saying that the years spoken of are lunar, and not solar. Draper points out, however, that this would be making them have children when **only** five or six years old.

The next great event that claims our attention, in investigating **the** character of the Hebrew legends, is the Deluge. I will **let** Mr. Shieffelin tell the story, since he does it so well, and puts forth the proofs so strongly, that I **feel** my inability **to improve** upon his account. Moreover, as I said before, he is not to be stayed by such a trifle as a scientific fact.

He says that it is probable that small boats had been built before the ark, though that vessel is the first one spoken of. So far I cordially agree with him. It is extremely probable. He draws a graphic picture of the ridicule cast upon the **work of building** this vast structure. He imagines one man saying, " He (Noah) thinks he is elected to be saved and the rest of the world is to be damned; I am thankful I don't believe in so unmerciful a God." This last is a touch of sarcasm. "The miracle," proceeds our author, " of all kinds of animals, birds, creeping things, etc., going 'two and two unto Noah into the ark,' must have caused some to wonder for a moment. Some may even have felt a little solemn, when all had gone in, with Noah and his wife, and his sons, and their wives; and the Lord had shut him in." All which sensations would have been, under the circumstances, highly natural and creditable. After describing the beginning of the great rain, and indulging in a little flight of fancy regarding the unsuccessful application of one of Noah's carpenters for admission into the ark, Mr. Shieffelin goes on to say, " In forty days the water had risen fifteen cubits, or about twenty-three feet, above the highest mountains, which would be, on an average, a rise of about 700 feet each day." I shall have a word to say about this presently.

Mr. Shieffelin is very sure that the Deluge took place. He says, " There is no fact in history better attested, independent of the word of God, than the flood; and none more universally acknowledged by all nations. Many evidences of it exist at the present day. The highest mountains, in every part of the earth where search has been made, furnish abundant proofs that the sea has spread over their summits; shells, skeletons of fish and sea monsters, being found on them. The universality of the flood is shown by the fact that the remains of animals are found buried far from their native regions. Elephants, natives of Asia and Africa, have been found buried in the midst of England; crocodiles, natives of the Nile, in the heart of Germany;

shell-fish never known in any but the American seas, and also skeletons of whales, in the most inland counties of England," etc.

The Deluge lasted forty days, and was then dried up by a wind. This story could only have originated with a people totally ignorant of the laws of the atmosphere, and the principles of hydrostatics. Its authors evidently supposed that rain came *de novo* from heaven. What are the actual facts? The amount of water on the earth, including the aqueous vapor in the atmosphere, is a constant quantity. Rain is simply the removal of a portion of this water from one part of the earth by evaporation, and its deposition in another. In consequence of gravitation, the great body of water, which we call the sea, occupies the lowest depressions of the globe. The rain which falls upon high levels, makes its way by water-courses down to the sea-level. In situations where it cannot immediately drain away, the overplus forms lakes, inland seas, etc. The Deluge must, therefore, have been composed of the water which was already upon the earth, and the "situation" at that time must have been as follows:

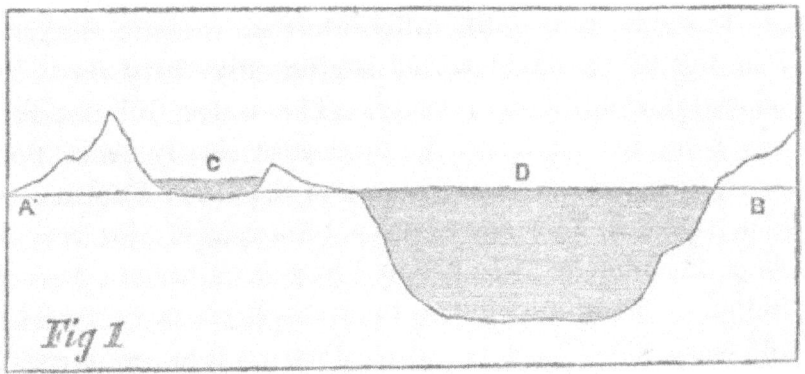

In Fig. 1 we have a supposed section of part of

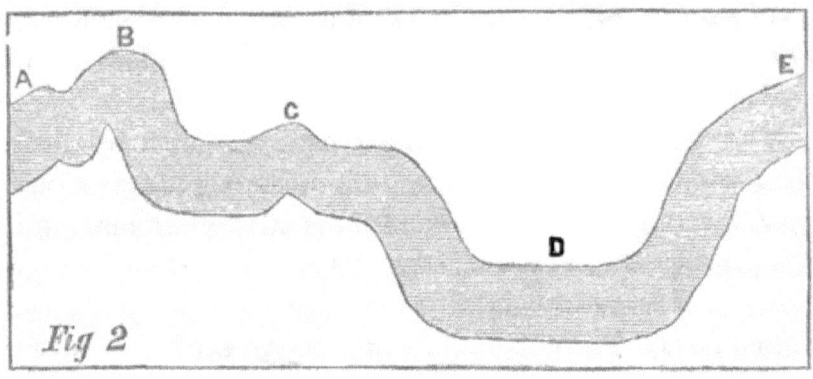

Fig 2

the globe, showing the present condition of things. A, B is the sea level, D the sea, and C a lake. Fig. 2 shows how this locality must have appeared at the Deluge, when the rain stayed where it fell, and the sea overflowed its banks. A, B, C, D, E indicates the position the water assumed under these circumstances.

A simple inspection of these two diagrams will make it clear that a general deluge is impossible so long as it is the tendency of water to run down hill.

It is true that the earth, during the silurian and part of the Devonian periods, was under water. That deluge, however, was quite different from the one spoken of in the Bible. Instead of lasting only forty days, it endured for millions of years. The water did not recede from the land, but the land rose slowly from the water, by a process of attrition and deposit. Successive submergences and emergences took place, the result being the deposition of one layer of alluvium above another. Ages of exposure to atmospheric and chemical influences have hardened that alluvium into solid rock, which still retains the skeleton relics of the animals and plants flourishing at the period of its formation. Mr.

Shieffelin shows his contempt for, or perhaps ignorance of, science in nothing more strongly than in his idea that the existence of fossils **proves** the account of the Flood. How the Deluge could not only have buried animals and plants **hundreds of** feet below the surface, **but** also have embedded them in solid stone, it is difficult to imagine.

The manner in which the Flood is said to have abated betrays an equal ignorance of natural laws. If such a mass of water *had* been spread over the earth, no wind could ever have dried it up. We should expect such a story from a primitive people, who, seeing a tubful of water dried up by wind, thought there was no limit to the powers of the latter in that direction. Let us, however, divest ourselves of the idea of gravitation, and imagine the **existence** of Noah's Deluge. The atmosphere would, as **it** does now, absorb aqueous **vapor up** to the point of saturation. When that was reached, the vapor would be precipitated again as rain. Inasmuch, **however, as** the water covers the entire globe, a shower falling on any portion of that liquid waste would raise the level (if I may use the term) not only of that part, but of the whole. We should have a succession of showers, but no abatement of the flood. Why does not the wind dry the ocean, which covers only a portion **of** the earth? Wind might have ruffled the surface of the Deluge, but could never have caused it to disappear.

There is usually a foundation of truth to a legend, and **I admit** that an extensive freshet may have given rise to that of **the Deluge, but it** could have been nothing more. That it was **not** universal (which I have shown to be ridiculous) can be proved from the record itself. The highest mountain in Western Asia is Ararat, upon which the ark is said to have rested. Its height is **given in** *Lippincott's Gazetteer* (from which work I **also take the** following figures) at 17,323 feet. The water, says **the account,** rose 23 feet higher, making in all 17,346 feet of depth. Now there are about forty peaks in the Himalaya range, whose height exceed 20,000 feet. **The** summit of Kunchainjunga is 28,178, that of Dhawalaghiri **28,000, and that of** Shumalari 23,929 feet above the sea. Many of the passes in these mountains are **more** than 20,000 feet high. There must, therefore, have been dry land more than 3,000 feet above the surface of the Flood, while some of the mountains towered above the watery expanse more than 11,000 feet. This is upon the supposition that the above-mentioned sounding of 23 feet was made exactly over Ararat. But how could the voyagers know they were in that spot when the sounding was taken? Even a maritime people would have been puzzled to be sure of that; while Noah and his family had confessedly lived inland, and knew no **more** of sea-going affairs than they did of the other side of the moon. The line would be thrown out anywhere, perhaps in a deep valley; and the assertion that it was over a mountain top would be entirely gratuitous. Moreover, for the reasons based upon gravitation which I have **given, the** water could never rise to a height of 17,346 feet, unless it refused to run down hill, which is not customary. Of course, a rise to that height on a level would **be still** more unreasonable, since there is only water enough upon the earth to reach to the line A, B in Fig. 1.

After the Deluge, the rainbow was given by God as a **sign** that a like catastrophe should never recur. This **shows** the childishness of the whole story. It is equivalent to asserting that at this time the properties of refraction and dispersion by dense media were bestowed upon light. But if these phenomena in the case of water are the " sign of promise," they must be equally so when manifested by flint glass. The spectroscope must be as much the " seal of the covenant" as the rainbow.

I have dwelt upon this story at some length, because it is a fair sample of a Bible legend. None of them will bear close examination; but all, when viewed without prejudice, and from the standpoint of common sense, will be found equally absurd. It seems strange that people who are undoubtedly shrewd in other respects, should put confidence in these fables. The explanation, I believe, may be found in the one-sided education to which they have been subjected, and their obedience to the priestly mandate, " Do not hear the other side."

The question may be asked, " Where did these stories, if they are not true, originate?" That question is now being answered. It was from the legendary lore of Persia and Assyria that the Jews drew the material for these astonishing narrations. The researches of Mr. George Smith in Assyria have brought to light many of the originals of the Bible legends, inscribed on the stone tablets of Nineveh and Babylon. Among these are the legend of the Deluge and that of the Tower of Babel. Now, if the Jewish books were written after the Assyrian captivity (and the evidence that this is the case is overwhelming), all doubt upon this subject should vanish at once.

Passing over the rest of these stories, therefore, let us go on to the prophets. I should stop for one moment, however, to speak of the Decalogue. I often hear the opinion expressed that the Ten Commandments must be of divine origin for two reasons: **first,** because they contain the sum of all justice; and secondly, because the human mind could never have deduced them unaided. Both these reasons are unfounded. The Decalogue **does not contain** all the principles of justice, nor pro**scribe every offense, by** a great deal. I am aware that theological ingenuity, by distorting the text of these precepts, has made them apparently cover more ground **than they** really do; but it is only by distortion **that** this result is attained. Thus the seventh commandment is made to forbid not only adultery, but obscene language; which **is** neither expresssed nor implied in the text. The reason given is that the latter leads to the former, which is untrue in the great majority **of** cases. Even after having undergone, however, **this** process of expansion, the Ten Commandments are exceedingly incomplete.

But while the Decalogue does not summarize all law **and** justice, it does contain one statement which is the very incarnation of injustice. This is, that the sins of the fathers shall be visited upon the children *unto the third and fourth generation.* A human tribunal which should condemn a man to punishment for the crimes of his father, would go down to posterity covered with infamy. Yet these words, the expression of the most vindictive malignity, are calmly attributed to the Almighty, of whom it is elsewhere said, " He doth not afflict wil**lingly."** Inconsistencies like this are too glaring to be explained away.

In answer to the second of the above reasons, **it may be said** that the unaided human mind **could conceive** such a code of laws, because it has done so in many instances. Exclusive of the hereditary justice clause, the precepts of the Decalogue are merely those at which every society arrives at an early period in its history. Nations who never heard of the Hebrews have founded their social system upon the rights of life and property, the prohibitions of religions other than their own, and, as they advanced somewhat in civilization, upon the sacredness of the family relation, and immunity from libel. The tendency of the human mind is always in certain definite directions, and hence the principles of justice are in all lands and all ages the same, though their mode of application may differ. In a primitive code, great crimes, which attract attention, would be provided for; while minor offenses, which form nine-tenths of the discord between man and man, would not be noticed. This is the case with the Decalogue. The refinements of law, designed to meet these cases, would not be added till at a later period in the history of the growing society.

I now come to speak of the prophets, a subject more vitally connected with the Christian religion than most of what I have gone over. With the exception of the legend of the Fall, all the marvelous stories of the Old Testament might be rejected without materially affecting Christianity. The Church is unwise to carry this worse than useless weight. But with the prophets it is different. Unless Jesus was a divinely sent personage, he could not be what his followers claim, and it is in the prophets that the proofs of this circumstance are said to be found. These proofs, Christians tell us, are that his advent is foretold, his character and mission described. Is this the fact?

At the present day, we are ignorant of the immediate circumstances under which many of the prophecies were written. No one can logically affirm, therefore, that they do not refer to contemporary events. Bearing this in mind, and also noting that none of the prophecies mention Jesus by name, to what conclusion are we led? Let us see. Suppose an ancient manuscript to be discovered in our own time, and suppose it is asserted that this manuscript contains a prediction of an event which has not yet taken place. Suppose, further, that this event is said to be the cessation of all vegetable life upon the earth. We take the document, and find the so-called prophecy to consist of a sentence following naturally with what precedes, and which, perhaps, reads thus: "Behold, the land is desolate, neither is there any green thing." A skeptic might say to a believer in the **prophecy**: "You tell me that this sentence refers to the extinction of vegetation, but that is only your imaginative construction. The sentence itself, so far from specifying **this** meaning, is so indefinite that you cannot logically assert that such is its significance. Besides, the words would apply perfectly well either to a drought or to a visitation of locusts, at the time they were written. Until, therefore, you can prove that no other meaning than the one you hold is possible, I shall believe that some such fact as I have mentioned gave rise to this passage. This I do not think you can do. It is not enough for you to show that the words may bear the interpretation you give them; you must demonstrate that they are ca**pa**ble of bearing no other. Between a rational and a supernatural explanation, I prefer to accept the rational; much more when the former suggests **itself at** once, and the latter is exceedingly far-fetched."

This line of argument applies fully to the prophecies of the Old Testament. Many of them obviously refer to occurrences mentioned in the record itself, and are in the past or present tense. Nay, more: passages which were not intended to be prophecies are yet called so by the Church. Such, for example, is that in which the author of the Twenty-second Psalm, speaking of the treatment he had received at the hands of his enemies, says, "They part my garments among them, and cast lots upon my vesture." Nothing but blind misunderstanding, or wilful imposture, could ever have erected this into a prophecy. It manifestly has reference to a contemporary event in the writer's own experience, not to an occurrence far in the future. Yet they tell us that it is a prediction of what happened at the crucifixion of Jesus, at which time the Roman soldiers divided his garments among them. As if that was not the custom of those gentry at every execution.

Another important point, at which I have before hinted, is the vagueness of the prophecies. This vitiates them for two reasons. In the first place, it is impossible to state positively that they refer to Jesus, since they apply equally well to thousands of other persons. In the second place, if they do refer to him, such is their indefiniteness that no one would so understand them at the time. It would require the occurrence of the event to show the meaning of the prophecy. And after an event has taken place, what is the use of a prediction? We may imagine man acting thus foolishly, but that God Almighty should amuse himself by such a device passes comprehension.

The prophets themselves were curious personages. They seem to have combined the functions of hermit, monk, and wandering minstrel. **Paine*** points out very clearly that at first the word "prophesy" meant to perform upon a musical instrument, and that the prophet was **at** that time a sort of troubadour. Thus, we read of a company of prophets prophesying with sackbuts, and there are numerous other such allusions. The soothsayers **were** then called seers (I Samuel ix, 9). Afterwards, however, the prophets assumed this latter office, and the two words came **to** signify the same thing. After the split in the Jewish nation, each party had its prophets, who mutually abused each other with **a fervor** worthy of modern Christian charity. Sometimes **one** side came out ahead, **and** sometimes **the** other. **They** also had family quarrels among themselves, as **in the** following instance, narrated in I Kings xxii.†

Jehoshaphat, King of Judah, and Ahab, **King of** Israel, had made common cause together **against** Syria, and were on the eve of the **siege** of Ramoth-Gilead. Before going into battle, however, they sent for a **number** of prophets, to inquire **of** them what would be the event of the engagement, just as others since that time have consulted fortune-tellers. The prophets, of course, recognizing their own interest, all predicted that the King of Syria would be defeated, and Ahab successful. Jehoshaphat was not quite satisfied with this unanimity. **It** wore rather too much the air of sycophancy. He, therefore, asked **if there** were **not still** another prophet of whom **they might inquire, to** make quite

---

* "Age of Reason," Part I.

† **To show** more clearly the significance of this and the following narrative, I have put them into modern language. That I have **in no** wise violated the spirit of the original, and very slightly **even** the letter, will be evident upon comparison.

sure. Ahab answered that there was Micaiah; "but," said he, "I hate him, for he doth not prophesy good concerning me, but evil." "Indeed," said Jehoshaphat, "you don't say so." Ahab, to show that it was really the case, sent for Micaiah, who evidently had a grudge against the other prophets, and did not particularly love the king. Micaiah came, and Ahab put to him the question, "Shall we go up to Ramoth-Gilead, or shall we forbear?" The prophet at once answered, "Go and prosper, for the Lord shall deliver it into the hand of the King." Ahab seems to have been surprised at the unwonted complaisance of Micaiah, and he conjured the latter not to deceive him, but to speak the truth. Micaiah resented this, as impugning his veracity, and accordingly took back his former utterance, and prophesied an overwhelming defeat. "I told you so," said Ahab quietly, turning to Jehoshaphat. But Micaiah was now in full career, and could not be stopped. He must have his fling at the other prophets. So he went on to state that in a vision he had heard the Lord ask who would persuade Ahab to go to Ramoth-Gilead and be killed. A spirit had answered that he would do it. The Lord asked him how. The demon replied, by becoming a lying spirit in the mouth of Ahab's prophets. Whereupon the Lord told him to go. Micaiah seems to have forgotten that he had at first prophesied the same as the rest, and that consequently he included himself in this category. Upon this Zedekiah, one of the maligned prophets, walked up to Micaiah, slapped his face, and asked him, "How long since the spirit of the Lord left me, to manifest itself to you?" "You shall know," retorted Micaiah, "when you are a fugitive, in fear for your life." Ahab was killed at Ramoth-Gilead, but no credit is due to Micaiah for the prediction, since he prophesied both ways.

Here was a pleasant state of things! These "men of God," as they were styled, evidently did not have a very high opinion of each other's pretentions. And I am content to take them at their own valuation.

An instance of the character of another class of their utterances occurs a little farther on (II Kings iii). Jehoram, the son of Ahab, was King of Israel, and was much troubled by the incursions of the King of Moab. He, therefore, besought Jehoshaphat to join with him in settling this troublesome neighbor. Jehoshaphat consented, and the two armies took up their march through the wilderness of Edom. While in that country the water supply gave out, and the army was greatly distressed in consequence. In this strait, Jehoshaphat inquired if there were not a prophet to whom they could apply for advice, and was told that there was Elisha. Elisha was accordingly sent for, and appeared. Seeing the King of Israel, however (he himself being of the party of Judah), and concluding that that monarch was the one who had summoned him, he exclaimed, "What made you send for me? Go to your own prophets." "Nay," said Jehoram, "never mind these differences now. We are perishing, and shall fall into the hands of our enemies." "As the Lord liveth," answered Elisha, "if it were not that I respect the presence of Jehoshaphat, King of Judah, I would have nothing to do with you." Having relieved his mind after this fashion, Elisha set to work to supply their great want. He first called for a minstrel to play before him, probably to give him time to think what to say. He then burst forth with, "Thus saith the Lord, make this valley full of ditches. For thus saith the Lord, ye shall not see wind, neither shall ye see rain; yet that valley shall be filled with **water**, that ye may drink." "This," observes Paine, "**was** what any countryman could have told them—that **the** way to get water was to dig for it."

I quote another instance, noticed specially by Paine, to show how the prophecies have been in many cases distorted from their obvious meaning, in order to make them apply to Jesus. The words are in Isaiah vii, and are as follows: "Behold, a virgin shall conceive, and bear a son, and shall call his name Immanuel." This passage is so constantly dissociated from its **context**, that I doubt not but many persons are ignorant of the connection in which it occurs. The circumstances were these: Rezin, King of Syria, and Pekah, King of Israel, had made war upon Ahaz, King of Judah. **The** allied forces were at this time besieging Jerusalem, but **were** unable to reduce the garrison. Isaiah, at this juncture, went to Ahaz, and told him in the name of the Lord that he should finally be victorious; directing him at the same time to ask a sign of the Lord, in proof of the truth of **this** assertion. Ahaz refused, saying that he would not tempt the Lord. Whereupon Isaiah rejoined, "Therefore the Lord himself shall give you a sign; behold, a virgin shall conceive, and bear a son, and shall call his name Immanuel. Butter and honey shall he eat, that he may know to refuse the evil, and choose the good. For before the child shall know to refuse the evil, **and** choose the good, the land **that** thou abhorrest shall be forsaken of both her **kings**." This puts quite a different face upon the matter. The birth of the child, and its refusing the evil and choosing the good, are to be a sign to Ahaz that he is to obtain the victory over Syria and **Israel, and, of course,** must occur before the latter event, as is expressly specified in the text. Moreover, a slight change must be made **in the** translation. The word virgin, in the original, **simply** means a young woman, and the tense is present, **not** future. What Isaiah said, therefore, was in effect this: "There is a young woman about to be delivered of a child. **N**ow, it shall be to you for a sign, that before this child shall know enough to **refuse** evil, and choose good (symbolized by his eating butter and honey), you shall prevail over Syria and Israel." **If we** turn to the next chapter we shall find that the child spoken of is the prophet's own. It would have been ridiculous to have given to Ahaz, as a sign of success, the promise that several centuries afterward Jesus should be **born.** The sign must be something that takes place before the event, and from which the latter may be known. But in prophesying victory to Ahaz, Isaiah was badly mistaken. The 28th chapter of II Chronicles tells us that Ahaz was defeated, with the loss of 120,000 men, 200,000 prisoners, and a large amount of spoil. So that even if this prophecy had referred to Jesus, it would be nullified. Such a meaning, however, could only be given to it **by forcibly** separating it from its connection.

None of the prophecies are better able to stand criticism **than** those I have mentioned. **If** they refer to Jesus, the language should be so unmistakable (the thing predicted being so important), that there could be no doubt about their meaning. In no instance, however, is this the case; while in regard to the majority, the application is most patently supplied by **the context,** as in the example given above. **We** may, therefore, taking also into account the character **of their authors,** of which I have quoted two illustrations, dismiss the prophecies as of no importance whatever.

I come now to speak of Jesus Christ, and I wish to do so with all possible respect. He was a great and good man. In the midst of narrowness, selfishness, and superstition, he preserved his nature, up to the time of his premature death, free from all these defects. He stands out prominently, through the genial freshness and grand simplicity of his character, a sun whose beams shall penetrate to the remotest ages of time. Long after Christianity has become one of the many extinct religions of earth, men will reverence the memory of Jesus Christ. It will therefore be understood that in what I am about to say, I am in no sense attacking the character of Jesus, but only the absurd mass of legend and superstition which has been imposed upon the world by the Christian Church, and by which the latter has obscured the brightness of its noble founder till it is almost eclipsed.

The first item in this Christian mythology, is the legend of Jesus' miraculous birth. He is said to have been born of a virgin. As he is also said, being God, to have taken upon himself a human nature in all respects like ours; and as none of us are born without a father, the story appears somewhat inconsistent with the latter statement. It is difficult to conceive how he could have been a man like ourselves, if he came into the world in that miraculous way. But let us examine into this a little further. Upon whose testimony does the accuracy of this account depend? Evidently upon his mother's, for she alone had the means of knowing. Now, this is not the only instance in which children have been born of unmarried women, nor indeed the only one in which such a story has been promulgated to account for the fact. Is it more likely that a pregnant unmarried female would tell an untruth to explain her condition, or that such an occurrence as the Immaculate Conception really took place? The inquiry becomes stronger when we remember that among a superstitious people, like the Jews, the belief in the story would not only remove the disgrace which would otherwise rest upon her, but actually exalt her importance.

Upon the whole, however, it is extremely improbable that Jesus was born out of wedlock. He is so often spoken of as Joseph's son, that it is probable that the legend of his miraculous birth did not arise till later—perhaps not until after his death. His genealogy as given by Luke (which differs fatally from that in **Matthew**), commences, "Jesus . . . being the son of Joseph, which was the son of Heli," etc. In this there have been inserted, evidently by a later hand, the words "as was supposed." I say by a later hand, for if he was not the son of Joseph, what has Joseph's genealogy to do with him? I cannot imagine Luke doing such a ridiculous thing as to give at length the line of Joseph, prefixing it by the remark that Jesus was not of this line. Moreover, if the wonderful story said to have been told by his mother had been made known previous to this, it would have spread all over the country, and he would *not* have been supposed to be Joseph's son.

The Gospels mention only one incident in the child**hood** of Jesus. This is that upon one occasion, at the **age of** twelve years, he was found by his parents in the Temple, listening to the doctors of the law, and asking them questions. This anecdote shows that even at that early period, he took a strong interest in the **Jewish** religion, which it was subsequently the labor of his life to reform. Further than this, we have no account of him until after he had arrived at man's estate, and was about to devote himself with all his strength to his self-appointed task. It is a grand spectacle to see a man thus daring openly to oppose the cherished ideas of ages, armed only with the sincerity of his convictions, and the magnanimity of his character, which make him a living example of the truths he teaches. Jesus stands before us in this position at the commencement of his public career. He is at first not without natural misgivings as to the result of his efforts, which are at times so strong that he is tempted to relinquish the work. He knows that he must encounter the odium of the priesthood and of the powerful Pharisees. He is **conscious** that in following the course he contemplates, he must resign all thoughts of wordly ambition. The kingdoms **of** this world and their glory will not be for him. Nor **are** these his only doubts. How is he to live? Can he command the stones to become bread? He is tossed about by these conflicting thoughts to such an extent that, in describing them at a later time to his disciples (who could have come by the knowledge in no other way), he speaks of them as a personal temptation of the Evil One. The disciples, who never understood **or** appreciated his character, accepted his words literally, **and** gravely narrated this as an actual occurrence.

At length his resolution is taken. There are higher needs in man's nature than that of meat and drink; and to the satisfaction **of these he will dedicate** his life. He must worship his heavenly Father, rather than the gods of this world, which perish. He therefore hesitates no longer, but enters at once upon his task, trusting for his daily bread to that loving and protecting Power without whose knowledge even the little sparrow does not fall to the ground. Ever afterwards in his teachings, this idea of dependence upon, and implicit confidence in, the Almighty, is the one most prominent. His highest praise was, "I have not found so great faith; no, not in Israel"; his most pathetic reproach, "O ye of little faith." Men had before conceived of God as a Lawgiver, a Judge; it was reserved for Jesus to depict him as the universal Father.

At first, all goes well. The common people receive him gladly, and follow him in crowds from place to place. His teachings fall upon the ears of the poor peasantry like the voice of the liberator speaking **to the** captive. Oppressed by priestly arrogance, ground down by religious exaction, this simple people hear with joy the words of one who tells them that these are but the vain inventions of men. When the Samaritan woman asks him whether Mount Gerizim or Jerusalem is the proper place to worship God, he replies, "Woman, believe me, the hour cometh when ye shall neither in this mountain, nor yet at Jerusalem, worship the Father. God is a spirit, and they that worship him must worship him in spirit and in truth." As if he had said, "God is not honored, but rather affronted, by all your petty insistance upon forms of ritual. A better day is coming, when men shall recognize that God is not a man that he should take delight in such sordid observances, but a spirit; and when they shall worship Him spiritually, for only so can he be worshiped in truth."

This is the key-note of Jesus' preaching. It is pure spiritism, coupled with an affectionate and trusting dependence upon his heavenly Father. **He does not** gather his hearers together in the synagogue **or temple,** but by the wayside, in the fields, and on the sea-shore. There, surrounded by the beauty and grandeur of God's handiwork, in that Church of Nature which modern Christians so despise, their Master drew in the inspiration for his sublime utterances. His most effective illustrations were taken from natural objects. "Consider the lilies," he exclaimed on one occasion, "they toil not, neither do they spin; and yet I say unto you that not even Solomon in all his glory was arrayed like one of these." In all his discourses this exuberant love of nature is apparent. From the above passage, he makes the following application: "Wherefore, if God so clothe the grass of the field, which to-day is, and to-morrow is cast into the oven, shall he not much more clothe you, O ye of little faith?" We may imagine the effect of such an appeal addressed to such an audience. No one **had** ever talked to them in this way before. They flock after Jesus in crowds, trying to touch even the hem of his garment. His path through Galilee is a continuous triumphal procession. At length, like all religious reformers, his enthusiasm makes him believe himself divinely called to the work he has chosen. He has so long thought of God as his Father, that he comes at last to regard himself as a specially favored son. In moments of ecstatic exaltation, he feels himself, like Plotinus and Porphyry, united to the Supreme Being. At one such time he exclaims, "I and my Father are one." The bystanders understood by this that he claimed equality with the Almighty; but he defended himself forcibly against a charge so repugnant to his nature. "Is it not," said he, "written in your law, I said, Ye are gods? If he called them gods unto whom the word of God came (and the scripture cannot be broken), say ye of him whom the Father hath sanctified and sent into the world, Thou blasphemest; because I said, I am **the** Son of God? If I do not the works of my Father, believe me not; but if I do, though ye believe me not, believe the works; that ye may know and believe that the Father is in me, and I in him." So far from claiming equality with God, he says expressly, "My Father is greater than I." In the face of this latter remark, the existence of such a doctrine as the **Trinity is somewhat** singular.

The ancient prophets had been fond of predicting the advent of a champion or Messiah, who should restore the Jewish nation to its grandeur during the reigns of David and Solomon. Jesus appropriates this idea, and announces that he also is the Messiah of a kingdom, but it is a kingdom not of this world. It is a kingdom whose seat is within a man, and in which whosoever will be greatest shall be made the servant of all. There must be no strife for power in this kingdom. It is to be the reign of love upon earth.

Filled with these ideas, Jesus, in the third year of his public life, goes to Jerusalem. The result was what might have been expected. No opponent of priestcraft is safe in a priest-ridden community if the power of the clergy extends to life and death. The outspoken denunciations of Jesus, his fresh, hearty scorn, made the hierarchs wince; and accordingly they hated him with an intensity of which the ungodly are not capable. **Jesus** was obliged to hide himself from their vengeance, but being at length betrayed by one of his own followers he was tried upon a frivolous charge, condemned, and executed. He died a victim to theological odium—a martyr to the principle of freethought in religion.

At this distance of time what estimate shall we form of the character of Jesus? A few considerations **will** help us, perhaps, in this task. Nothing can be more certain than that if his counterpart should arise to-day, his bitterest and most unrelenting enemies would be the Christian Church. He was what is called in this age a leveler. He believed in no doctrine because it was old; he had respect for no opinion because it was held by the great ones in the synagogue or nation. He judged every custom, every tradition, every dogma entirely upon its own merits, and most found them he of sadly wanting. He had for all priestly machinery an undisguised indignation and contempt. "Woe unto you," said he, "for ye bind heavy burdens, grievous to be borne, and lay them on men's shoulders; but ye yourselves will not touch them with one of your fingers." If he were to reappear in this nineteenth century in our **country,** no one would reprobate more strongly than he the mass of superstition, Pharisaism, and spiritual tyranny which has been imposed upon the world in his name—in *his* name whose sole object in life was to protest against these very things! As well preach despotism in the name of Washington. Before he had been long among us he would find himself condemned as unorthodox. If he still persisted in his irreligious teachings, the Christians of to-day would, like the Jews of old, exclaim as one man, "Crucify him! Crucify him!"

I have thus briefly sketched the man as prefatory to touching upon the remaining absurdities of the system named after him. It will be better to take these up generically rather than specifically. Proceeding upon this plan, we first encounter the **subject** of miracles. The miracles attributed to Jesus are by no means the only ones we meet with in ancient writings, both sacred and profane. The same line of reasoning, however, **of** course applies to all.

Whatever explanation be given of miracles, of one thing we may rest assured—they never took place as reported. A miracle is, by direct implication, an occurrence which is in direct opposition to natural laws. If it be merely in conformity to laws which chance to be unknown, it is not a miracle. To be such, it must **be** antagonistic to all law. Now we have only one method by which the economy of **nature may be** truly ascertained, and that is the one spoken of at the commencement of this essay—observation and induction. The course of reasoning is often called the argument from experience. We must observe a large number of facts— the larger the better—and from these we may generalize to the law. What are called laws of nature are merely such generalizations of phenomena, and may be compared to those algebraic formulæ which are constructed to include a great number of cases in one comprehensive proposition. The product of $x + y$ multiplied by itself is always $x^2 + 2xy + y^2$, though to x and y be given any values whatsoever. In the same manner, instead of enumerating all the different bodies which, left without support, fall **to the** earth, we say generally that all bodies thus fall. It is necessary to make this explanation, because the clergy often talk as if natural law were a pure invention of the atheistic intellect.

Bearing in mind the above definition, the student of nature cannot fail to note, in all her manifestations, the inflexibility of these laws. This **is** so universal, that the result of any particular experiment upon a known law can be with absolute certainty predicted. **If I hold** a weight in my hand, and then let it go, I know beyond a doubt what will happen. The weight will certainly fall. No one has ever seen an exception to this law. There is no such thing in nature as exception to law. To take an instance often referred to in this connection, let us glance at the discovery of Neptune. It had been observed that the motion of Uranus was not what it had been computed to be from theory. But astronomers did not suppose for a moment that here was an exception to the principle of gravitation. On the contrary, having unlimited confidence in the universality of that principle, they reasoned that there must be an unknown body producing the disturbance. They calculated, upon the basis of the theory, the place and mass of the disturbing body; they looked for it in that place, and there they found it. This discovery was a triumphant establishment of the all-pervasiveness of the reign of law. We cannot, therefore, say that the laws of nature may be controverted, because we have absolutely no data upon which to base such an assertion; all observation leading to directly the opposite conclusion.

The idea of miracles arises from the mode before referred to, of attempting to explain natural phenomena—namely, the appeal to consciousness. It is based upon the *a priori* supposition that the universe is governed by an arbitrary personal intelligence—a Big Man. **Of course** to such a being, acting merely from caprice, miracles, in the ordinary sense, would be possible. In that case, however, they would not really be miracles; for, nature not being under the rule of law, any departure from her ordinary method is no more wonderful than adherence to that method. But how does it happen, upon this hypothesis, that we have method in nature at all?

That all observation contradicts this view is no obstacle to its supporters. The latter are accustomed to disparage reason as something which leads mankind only into error, unless "aided"—in other words, hampered—by *a priori* conceptions which are the death of all intellectual progress.

Taking the Calvinistic view of God, miracles are clearly impossible. "God," says Calvinism, "can do anything." Can he, then, sin? No, for that is contrary to the very idea of God. What is sin? The Westminster Catechism tells us that "sin is any want of conformity unto, or transgression of, the law of God." It is admitted, therefore, that God rules by means of law. Now, inasmuch as a miracle would be *both* out of conformity with, *and* in transgression of, some portion of the law of God, it must be conceded that God would sin if he performed a miracle.

Upon a rational basis, it is easy to see the origin of these reputed miracles. "No miracle," says Renan, "was ever performed before a people who did not believe in miracles." In this eminently true remark we have the core of the whole matter. Given a superstitious people, as were all the ancients, the Jews included, and the genesis of these legends needs no further exposition. Testimony is never wanting to support the supernatural. We have only to glance, in confirmation of this, at so comparatively recent a set of occurrences as the trials for witchcraft in Massachusetts. Read the sworn evidence of witnesses to the effect that witches in the shape of black cats, etc., appeared to them and conversed with them, and then place any confidence, if you can, in other similar testimony. If such things happened in modern times, what shall we expect of former ages, when the existence of the marvellous was not even questioned? We must also recollect that other miracles besides those found in the Bible are just as well authenticated as the latter. It would be extremely illogical to accept the miracles of Jesus, and reject the legends of the saints, which rest upon just as strong a foundation. McCosh* sees an essential difference in character between the miracles of Jesus, and those of Simon Magus, for example. The latter is said to have flown through the air, rolled himself unhurt upon burning coals, caused statues to talk, etc. Inasmuch as Jesus is reported to have walked upon the water, conjured money into a fish's mouth, passed through closed doors, and done numerous other similar acts, I fail to discern McCosh's distinction.

The resurrection of Jesus from the dead is the sheet-anchor of Christianity. It is a pity the accounts of it do not agree better. One evangelist says that Mary Magdalene and another woman came to the sepulcher, when they saw an angel descend from heaven, roll back the stone from the entrance, and sit upon it. The angel told them that Jesus had risen. Another asserts that when the women arrived at the tomb, they found the stone already removed, and a young man sitting inside the sepulcher. A third testifies that they found the tomb empty, and, while they were wondering thereat, two men in shining garments suddenly stood by them; while the fourth gives as his version that Mary Magdalene, Peter, and himself were the ones who went to the sepulcher, which they found empty. Peter and John

---

* "Christianity and Positivism," p. 289.

then went their way, and after Mary was left alone she saw two angels inside. Mark says that the women said nothing to any man of what they had seen, because they were afraid; while Luke declares that they told the eleven and all the rest. So that the several accounts even of so momentous an event as the resurrection, are fatally discrepant. Of course, the resurrection, being a miracle, comes under the observations already made on the general subject. In this case, however, the origin of the story is quite apparent. If we compare the different accounts, we shall find that the only character who figures in them all is Mary Magdalene. It is upon her testimony that the legend of the resurrection rests. It is not at all unlikely that an enthusiastic woman would devise such a report. She also was the first who saw him alive again. It would not be difficult to find some one to personate for a few days the character of Jesus, and then disappear in order to give rise to the report of the ascension. This view is supported by the fact that no one seems to have recognized Jesus subsequent to the resurrection, until he disclosed himself to them. Upon one occasion the representative of Jesus walked several miles with two disciples who had followed the Master daily, and yet they did not know him. This could hardly be if it were really Jesus. Moreover, Jesus risen from the dead would have nothing to fear from the utmost publicity, which it would rather be his object to court. His representative, on the contrary, skulks among the back ways of Jerusalem, and makes appointments to meet the apostles in secluded and out-of-the-way places. It does not appear that any excitement was caused among the populace by the resurrection. In regard to the ascension, also, accounts **differ.** Matthew and John say nothing about it. **Mark and Luke dispose** of it in about a dozen words, and even **then contradict** each other. The one says the ascension took place from a room where the eleven sat at meat, and the other that Jesus led them out as far as Bethany and was there parted from them.

But why reason gravely concerning what is legendary **and** absurd upon its very face? For no other reason than to show that those who profess, or are asserted, to narrate the circumstance under the effect of inspiration, do not tell a straight story. In a court of justice, such conflicting testimony would ruin any cause. Of course, if the different narratives fitted each other as neatly as the parts of a machine, the legend would still be utterly unworthy the credence of a rational man. Its situation is much worse, however, **when** it has not even consistency to recommend it.

We find in the Acts of the Apostles some incidents set forth which remind us of the Old Testament. The punishment of Ananias and Sapphira is one of these. It **needs no** comment. With such a story currently believd, no one would venture to " keep back part of **the price** " in future. We also find an account of **certain fiery** tongues descending upon the apostles, by which they were enabled to speak all languages without having learned them. If their Greek is a specimen, it was not much of a gift. These tongues were said to be the Holy Ghost. The conversion of Paul, the story of the serpent that fastened upon his arm, and numerous other similar occurrences mentioned in the **book of Acts, all** have the genuine old ring to them. **What has been said** of former anecdotes of the same kind, applies equally well to these.

The subject of prayer is one that has recently attracted

considerable attention. Like the kindred topic, miracles, it is inconsistent with the idea of law. If there is an arbitrary personal intelligence at the head of natural events, of course requests made to that power may meet with a response. But if, as all observation plainly teaches, everything that happens is the result of law, and the condition of nature at any moment is the direct resultant of its condition at the previous moment, then prayer is a waste of breath. In purely physical affairs (so called) its fruitlessness is particularly apparent. Take, as an oft-quoted example, the prayer for rain. The physical facts connected with rain are briefly these: an area of low barometer moves over a certain locality, its motion being subject to law, and capable of being predicted; the surrounding air then rushes in to restore the equilibrium. Now, if the air comes from a warm quarter, or from over the ocean, it will be charged with moisture; and the expansion it undergoes upon coming into the region of diminished pressure, causes that moisture to condense in the form of clouds which fall in rain. If the wind blow from a very cold quarter, the moisture already present in the locality in question is chilled and condensed thereby, and a similar result follows. It is also capable of prediction, in any instance, from what point of the compass the wind will blow, so that the weather can be foretold for twenty-four or forty-eight hours in advance. All this plainly shows that atmospheric phenomena are not exempt from the universal legislation of nature. No entreaty of man can alter the sequence of these events in the slightest degree. Of course, if a man prays for rain, and persists in his prayer till the rain comes, he gets what he wants. Inasmuch, however, as the rain would have come in any case, it may reasonably be doubted whether the prayer had much to do with it. Prayer is a tacit assertion that the order of nature **may** be changed at man's request, which is placing it so far under his control. Every candid man is aware that in his own case this is not true, and yet many are unwilling to deny, in the aggregate, what each, in detail, knows to be false.

In 1872, Sir Henry Thompson proposed to the religious community to make this matter of prayer the subject of a test, with a view of ascertaining its exact value. I have now before me the text of this famous "prayer-gauge," commonly, though erroneously, attributed to Tyndall. Sir Henry selects, as the subject of inquiry, the prayer for the sick. His proposition is, to take a single hospital, supplied with the best professional attendance, and devoted to diseases whose pathology and death-rate are best known, and make it the **object of** special prayer by the faithful for a period of, say, five years. At the end of that time the mortality statistics are to be compared with previous results in the same hospital, and in other similarly well-managed institutions, and thus the value of prayer will be determined. Here was the Church's opportunity. Nothing could be fairer than this proposition. Either prayer for the sick is of value, or it is not. If it is, here is a simple, straightforward, and conclusive plan of demonstrating the fact. If prayer cannot furnish such a demonstration, it is a mere figment of the imagination, taking its rise in that superstitious tendency to which I have already referred.

The community waited anxiously for the action of the clergy upon the proposal. What was the result? *They refused to allow the experiment to be tried.* For this conduct various reasons were assigned, all equally frivolous. Such prayer would not be made in the proper spirit; it would be an insult to the Almighty, etc. In fact, they surrounded the subject of effectual prayer with so many conditions that, as no man could ever fulfil them all, prayer "in the proper spirit" became an impossibility. A man must be as resigned to the refusal of his prayer, as to its being granted. This is saying in effect, that in order for him to get what he wants, he must not desire it sufficiently to care whether he gets it or not; —a state of mind somewhat difficult to imagine. If it would be an insult to the Almighty to place beyond question his willingness to answer the requests of his people, then this proposition was an insult; otherwise, not. We read in the Bible* that Elijah tried a similar experiment, and met with divine approval. It cannot, therefore, be impious to repeat the test at the present day. The real reason for the refusal of the clergy was the secret conviction in their own minds, albeit some would not admit it to themselves in so many words, that prayer would not stand even such a simple test. But if that is the case, its value is purely imaginary.

Running away before a battle, however, is equivalent to confessing oneself beaten. To all intents and purposes, therefore, the experiment *was* tried, and resulted in defeat for the Church. "He that doeth truth, cometh to the light, that his deeds may be made manifest, that they are wrought in God."†

Many of the clergy are wise enough to see that prayer has no value in physical affairs. They therefore relegate it to the domain of the mind, or soul. Here the phenomena are so complex that it seems at first

---

* I Kings xviii, 17 *et seq.* † John iii, 21.

sight as if law had no place in this realm. But in reality it is not so. The laws of the mind are being gradually discovered, and are found to be as rigid as those in any other province of nature. Every resolve, every emotion, every thought, happens as much through the action of law as the lightning or the tempest. "There is no such thing," says Draper, with epigrammatic truth, "as a spontaneous or self-originated thought."* It can be foretold at the beginning of any year how many persons in a given community will be dishonest during the year, how many will commit suicide, etc. Of the suicides it can be predicted what proportion will drown themselves, how many blow their brains out, how many take poison, and so on. Law is everywhere—there is no room for prayer in any department of nature.

The doctrines of the resurrection of the body, and of the future state, complete the Christian scheme. As to the first, it is an exceedingly clumsy device. After a man dies, his body returns to the earth, and becomes distributed through the substance of other bodies, and of vegetation. If the body be burned, it is more quickly decomposed than if buried. At the resurrection, therefore, not only would the particles of the body have to be gathered together out of rock, plant, and animal, but as every particle would have formed part of more than one body, the question would arise to which it belongs. The originators of this dogma were evidently ignorant of what is called secular change. The matter which has furnished bodies to the earth's population through all

---

* While speaking of protoplasm, I used the word "self-originated," as applied to impulses. The term was there employed in a conventional, not in an exact, sense.

ages, would not simultaneously supply half of them. Many poor souls would be left out in the cold, so to speak. The resurrection of the body, apart from its mythical character, is a scientific impossibility.

The Egyptians, from whom this notion was derived, followed it up more logically. They preserved the body, in order that the spirit might find it intact, even if slightly dry, when it should be wanted. Christians do not do this, and even the labor of the Egyptians is, after thousands of years, fast becoming of no avail, since the mummies are being consumed as fuel on the railroads of modern Egypt.

Closely allied to the doctrine of the resurrection is that of a future state. This implies the idea of spirit. The hypothesis of the existence of spirit (by no means peculiar to, or orignating with, Christianity) supposes that there is in every human being an immaterial part, which is really the man himself. To this the body stands in the relation of a house to its tenant. The body may, and does, die; but the spirit is immortal. For every child born into the world a soul is created. It is the soul that thinks, feels, and suffers; the body is merely its minister.

Modern research on the subject of the nervous system is fast putting this idea to flight; still, however, our theme would not be complete without some allusion to it. If the doctrine be true, the spirit must enter into a child at some definite time. When does this time occur? If at the ordinary period of birth, how is it with seven months' children? If these latter have souls, how about the fœtus at six months? at five? at four? We continue our inquiries until we reach at last the ovum. But this is merely a protoplasm cell, not differing from those we may draw up from the ocean depths. It is impossible to conceive of an immortal soul residing in a minute globule of albuminoid substance. Still, one of my opponents may reply, it is perhaps so. Then it must be conceded that all protoplasm cells have souls; and, as the human body contains myriads of these, a man must have a corresponding number of souls. If we glance at the life of a human being, we find that at birth this part that thinks and feels is rudimentary and undeveloped. As the body increases in size and strength, this also correspondingly increases. When the body arrives at perfect development, the soul is at its prime. This stage past, the body begins to be enfeebled, the soul keeping exact pace with it. The body at length becomes helpless, the senses fail, and the entire system shows plainly that it is nearly exhausted. The soul is not more vigorous than its companion. The mental powers are nearly gone, memory has lost her seat, the reasoning faculties are dimmed. At last, the worn-out body dies, and the soul?—springs at once into life and vigor, says the Church. Where is there one single fact in the past history of soul and body to lead to such a conclusion? Does not everything contradict it? If the brain becomes injured, the mind or soul is correspondingly impaired. If, therefore, the brain dies, what then? There was exhibited in New York a few years ago, a negro girl with two heads. The cause of this phenomenon was evidently the fusing together of two fœtuses at an early stage of intra-uterine life. There was but one set of digestive and respiratory organs, rather larger than ordinary, as might have been expected. Both brains were active, and one head could talk upon one subject, while the other discoursed upon another. In fact, this girl had two souls; and why ? Because **she** had two brains. The residence of the soul, therefore, **is the** brain, and only by means of this organ does it manifest itself. In the event of the absence or death of the brain, how does the soul exist ? Questions like these are difficult, —nay, impossible—for the spiritist to answer, and are increasing in number every day. Moreover, though a child be born of shame, or even of crime, God is obliged to create for it a soul. This is plainly making the Almighty subservient to the worst passions of mankind.

As this doctrine did not originate with Christianity, the Church is to be held responsible for it only so far as she gives it her support. It is not intellectually pernicious, like most of the Christian myths; it is simply untenable. Its poetic beauty will not save it from the inevitable fate of error.

A few words before closing upon the past and present attitude of the Church toward progress. It has been, and is, an attitude of steady opposition. In the early **centuries** of our era, when Church and State were one, the means taken to suppress enlightenment were the dungeon, the rack, the cruel torture, and the stake. As a natural consequence, during the ten centuries' sway of the Church, the world groped in intellectual darkness. The revival of learning in the sixteenth century was simultaneous with the decadence of priestly rule. Always imitating, however, the conduct of those who love darkness rather than light because their deeds are evil, the Church still opposes, with equal hostility, though with greatly diminished power, every attempt to lead the race **to** a higher intellectual plane. At the present **time, the policy** pursued is one of insidious treachery. The clergy **profess the greatest** respect for science, and even devote their personal attention thereto. They claim the right to judge, however, between true and false science; and tell us that the former deals only with ascertained facts, not with wild speculations and theories. By the latter phrase is always meant evolution in some form—Darwinism, or the nebular theory. Now, inasmuch as the same line of reasoning would have applied equally well to gravitation, or the undulatory theory, when these were yet in abeyance, the principle if put in force soon enough would have checked all intellectual growth whatsoever. There is no mental pleasure in the mere observation of facts, if the mind is forbidden to generalize and draw inferences therefrom. Accordingly, if we followed the teachings of the Church in regard to science, the latter would speedily die for want of breath; and this is exactly the result which, under the guise of friendship, is aimed at. But forewarned is forearmed, and it is exceedingly doubtful if the Church, now herself upon the defensive, can ever re-establish her tyranny over the minds of men.* It is true that science positively sanctions nothing that has not been definitely ascertained, but she reserves to herself the right of judgment; and meanwhile gives a provisional consent to that theory which is best supported. Science holds to nothing after it has been proved to be false, but I challenge any one to point to an instance in which she has retired defeated from a contest with the Church. Whatever enlightenment may exist in this nineteenth century we owe entirely to science. In the face of all history to the contrary, it is impertinence to claim for Christianity the credit of modern civilization.

---

* A great point was gained when science was introduced into the colleges, of course after bitter clerical opposition.

In conclusion, I wish to address a few words of earnest appeal to the vast majority of the Christian laity, who are members of the Church because of their education, or who have joined under the influence of religious excitement. My petition to these persons is (and I would I could urge it more strongly), Hear the other side. If your religion be what you believe it is, the revelation of God to man, you have nothing to fear from any assaults made upon it. There have been and are now, as you know, men of culture and intellectual renown who think differently from you. You have heard these men villified, and are perhaps ready to join in condemning them to infamy. Have you forgotten that mob in the city of Jerusalem, who, when asked, " What evil hath this man done?" had no reply to give save, " Let him be **crucified**"? Do you desire to make such conduct your **own?** Did it never occur to you that these men whom you despise might possibly have been sincere in what they said and wrote? Has the thought not passed through your mind that they may perhaps have had better reason for their belief than you have for yours, inasmuch as they have done what you have not—given the subject an investigation? Does not your sense of justice recoil from meting out condemnation to those whom you have given no chance to speak? Let me beg you, in the name of fairness, to persist in this course no longer. Truth has no need of suppression and prejudice. You would not approve the conduct of a juror who made up his mind after hearing one side of a case. But what you would condemn in such a man you are yourself practic**ing in** regard to a matter whose issue is infinitely more momentous. Nay, more: the chances are that you could not even defend from attack your own side. If you could converse with Paine or Voltaire upon this subject, you would probably be vanquished. **Put on** your armor, therefore, and qualify yourself to "give a reason for the hope that is in you." But you will tell me, perhaps, that your clergyman has examined the arguments of skeptics, and has told you from the pulpit, or in private, that they are frivolous, that a child can answer them, and so on. My friend, allow no one to think for you in this matter. If you wished to ascertain whether charges against a public official were well grounded, you would not accept their denial by the party implicated as conclusive. If you will read the arguments your spiritual adviser makes so light of, you will find that they are anything but frivolous, and that a child could by no means answer them. Indeed, you must be aware that the acutest intellects in your Church have not thought it beneath them to engage in this discussion. If you are a Roman Catholic, my words are **not** meant for you, because your Church forbids freedom **of** opinion. But if you are a Protestant, exercise that right of individual judgment which is the corner-stone of Protestantism. Read first the arguments **on** your own side, in order that you may know with exactness what you do profess. Read next the arguments of the opposition, that you may be capable of forming an opinion upon the whole case. You must view it on all sides before you can do that. Until you do it, you "worship you know not what." But you have no time to **do all** this? Then you have no time to believe one side or the other. Would you **sign a** document of whose contents you were ignorant, if you had no time to **read** it? Yet **that** is what you are doing here.

Do not let prejudice govern you in this discussion.

There is an infallible means of determining whether you are under its sway. If you find yourself regarding any opinion, or any argument, with horror or shrinking, you may be sure that you are still prejudiced, and not in a condition for your judgment to act calmly.

Lastly, do not allow your inclinations to influence your final decision. Accept those opinions which your reason tells you are best supported by evidence, giving to every argument its full weight. If the opposition appears to you to have the best of the case, admit it like a man. There is no cowardice so contemptible as being afraid to believe what one's conscience tells him is true. If the result is otherwise, you will then have what you certainly have not now—an intelligent belief in the doctrines of Christianity. In either event you will have the satisfaction of knowing that you have acted honestly with yourself, as you believe you must finally act in the great **Day** of Judgment.

PUBLICATIONS OF CHARLES P. SOMERBY.

Prometheus. "*To Destroy, you must Replace.*" PROMETHEUS is a Journal designed as an aid to the Reconstruction of Society on the basis of the Philosophy of Science. It gives prominence to the best efforts of Constructive Thinkers in Europe. It is also a Weekly Record and Review of the best and latest Philosophical, Scientific, Oriental, and Rationalistic Literature, and contains a Select List of these works. An octavo weekly. **$3 per year, in** advance, postpaid ; single copy, 10c.

The Martyrdom of Man. By WINWOOD READE. Extra cloth, 12mo, 543 pp. Postpaid, $3.

It is really a remarkable book, in which universal history is " boiled down" with surprising skill.—[Literary World.

The sketch of early Egyptian history, in the first chapter, is a masterpiece of historical writing. He has a style that reminds us of Macaulay.—[Penn Monthly.

Nathaniel Vaughan. A Novel. By FREDERIKA MACDONALD, author of the "Iliad of the East," etc. 3 vols. in 1, extra clo., black and gold side stamp, 12mo, 404 pp. Postpaid, $1.50.

An independent and respectable study of character in the law of circumstance such as even George Eliot might not have been ashamed to own. . . . It is a really artistic composition, with a sound moral expressed, though not obtruded, on the canvas.—[Westminster Review.

A Few Words About the Devil, and Other Biographical Sketches and Essays. By CHARLES BRADLAUGH. Portrait, 2d ed., extra cloth, gold side stamp, 12mo, 260 pp. Postpaid, $1.50.

In a handsome volume before us Charles Bradlaugh has " A Few Words " to say " About the Devil." Mr. Bradlaugh has a right to his Few Words, and the Devil will, we presume, at no distant day, have a " few words ' to say to Mr. Bradlaugh, and will doubtless get the best of the argument.—[Chicago Interior.

Issues of the Age; Or, Consequences Involved in Modern Thought. By HENRY C. PEDDER. Extra cloth, beveled, gold back and side stamp, 12mo. Postpaid, $1.50.

The **author of** this volume has evidently kept company with many of the finer spirits of the age, until his mind has become imbued with the fragrance of their thought. He has excellent tendencies, elevated tastes, and sound aspirations.—[New York Tribune.

The Politics of the Gospels; Or, the Socialistic Element in the Early Christian Movement. By AUSTIN BIERBOWER. Extra cloth, 12mo. Postpaid, $1.50.

An interesting statement of the Socialistic ideas, tendencies, and purposes of the primitive Christians.

The Christ of Paul; Or, the Enigmas of Christianity. St. John never in Asia Minor ; Iræneus the author of the Fourth Gospel ; the Frauds of the Churchmen of the Second Century Exposed. By GEORGE REBER. Extra cloth, 12mo, 400 pp. Postpaid, $2.

The purpose of this book is to convince the world that the greater part of the New Testament, as at present received by Christians, was fabricated by the dogmatists of the second century, to enforce doctrines which were not warranted by the original teachings of Christ and the Apostles.—[New York Daily World.

Send for Complete Descriptive List.

CHARLES P. SOMERBY, Publisher,

139 Eighth Street, New York.

PUBLICATIONS OF CHARLES P. SOMERBY.

Heroines of Freethought. By Sara A. Underwood. Large new type, heavy tinted paper, broad margins. Extra cloth, 12mo, 327 pp. Postpaid, $1.50.

A series of brief biographies of the most distinguished Freethinking women of the past and present centuries, including Madame Roland, Mary Wollstonecraft Godwin, Harriet Martineau, Frances Power Cobbe, George Eliot, and half a dozen others.

Personal Immortality, and Other Papers. By Josie Oppenheim. Extra cloth, 12mo, about 100 pp. Postpaid, $1.

A woman's modest and considerate statement of her dissent from current theological ideas—in which Immortality and Prayer are discussed with ability, from a standpoint of pure Rationalism.

The Historical Jesus of Nazareth. By M. Schlesinger, Ph.D., Rabbi of the Congregation Anshe Emeth, Albany, N. Y. Extra cloth, 12mo, 98 pp. Postpaid, $1.

This little volume of less than a hundred pages contains what a conscientious and learned Jew of the nineteenth century has to say about Jesus Christ as an historical figure and character.—[St. Louis Republican.

The Ultimate Generalization. An Effort in the Philosophy of Science. Extra cloth, 12mo, 56 pp. Postpaid, 75 cents.

The statement, accompanied by strong evidence, of a new law named "Correlation," larger or more inclusive than that of Evolution; claimed to be the ultimate inductive basis of the Philosophy of Science, and by implication to have a bearing more or less direct upon all the great questions of the time.

The Case Against the Church. A Summary of the Arguments against Christianity. "*Not giving heed to Jewish fables.*"—Titus i, 14. Extra cloth, 12mo, 72 pp. Postpaid, 75 cents.

An attempt is here made to apply the principles of scientific materialism to the investigation of the myths and legends of Christianity.

Advancement of Science. Tyndall's Belfast Inaugural Address, and the Famous Articles of Professor Tyndall and Sir Henry Thompson ON PRAYER. With Portrait and Biographical Sketch of Professor Tyndall. And opinions of his services by the eminent scientist Professor H. Helmholtz. Postpaid, paper, 35 cents; cloth, 75 cents. Inaugural and portrait, paper, 15 cents.

Professor Tyndall has inaugurated a new era in scientific development, and has drawn the sword in a battle whose clash of arms will presently resound through the civilized world.—[New York Tribune.

Essays on Mind, Matter, Forces, Theology, Etc. By Charles E. Townsend. Extra cloth, 12mo, 404 pp. Postpaid, $2.

The author advances some novel theories on theological and scientific questions, leading to somewhat original conclusions.

The Safest Creed, and Twelve other Recent Discourses of Reason. By O. B. Frothingham. Cloth, beveled, black side stamp, 12mo, 238 pp. Postpaid, $1.50.

"To cherish no illusion" might be the text of every one of them. There is everywhere a resolute attempt to adjust thought and life to what is really known, to accept the facts and then see what sustenance can be extracted from them.—[Liberal Christian.

Send for Complete Descriptive List.

CHARLES P. SOMERBY, Publisher,
139 Eighth Street, New **York.**

PUBLICATIONS OF CHARLES P. SOMERBY.

The Cultivation of Art, And its Relations to Religious Puritanism and Money-Getting. By A. R. COOPER. 12mo, postpaid, fancy paper, 50 cents; flexible cloth, 75 cents.

It is not religion, but religion's parody, theology, which arrays itself in opposition to that sincere and manifold expression of human impulse and power to which we give the name of art.—[Extract.

The Essence of Religion. God the Image of Man. Man's Dependence upon Nature the Last and Only Source of Religion. By L. FEUERBACH, author of "Essence of Christianity." Cloth, 12mo. Postpaid, 75 cents.

The purpose of my writing is to make men *anthropologians* instead of *theologians*; man-lovers instead of God-lovers; students of this world instead of candidates for the next; self-reliant citizens of the earth instead of subservient and wily ministers of a celestial and terrestrial monarchy.—[Feuerbach.

The Childhood of the World. A Simple Account of Man in Early Times. By EDWARD CLODD, F.R.A.S. 12mo. Postpaid, paper, 50 cents; cloth, 75 cents.

Information not popularly accessible elsewhere as to the life of Primitive Man and its relation to our own.—[E. B. TYLOR, F. R. A. S.

Soul Problems. With Papers on the Theological Amendment and the State Personality Idea. By JOSEPH E. PECK. 12mo. Postpaid, paper, 50 cents.

The author is a materialist. He holds that matter is the only entity, that personal, conscious immortality is impossible; that that which is born must die—that which is formed must be dissolved. He is mild in his plea, has no epithets for the believers, and presses his cause only by argument.

The Antiquity of Christianity. By JOHN ALBERGER. 12mo. Postpaid, paper, 35 cents; cloth, 75 cents.

The Divine Origin of Christianity Disproved by its Early History. The Confessions of the Church Fathers as to the Paganism of their Creed.

Positivist Primer. Conversations on the Religion of Humanity. Dedicated to the only Supreme Being man can ever know; the Great, but Imperfect, God, HUMANITY, in whose image all other Gods were made, for whose service all other Gods exist, and to whom all the Children of Men owe Labor, Love, and Worship. Cloth, 12mo. Postpaid, 75 cents.

Religious Positivism. A Brief Exposition of the System of Worship, of Faith, and of Life, Propounded by Auguste Comte. Love our Principle, Order our Basis, Progress our End." By H. EDGER. Paper, 12mo. Postpaid, 50 cents.

Scripture Speculations. With an Introduction on the Creation, Stars, Earth, Primitive Man, Judaism, etc. By HALSEY R. STEVENS. Extra cloth, 12mo, 419 pp. Postpaid, $2.

He approaches his subject with all reverence, with a mind well stored with the facts of modern speculation and discovery, and in a modest and independent spirit. He writes with great candor and freedom, and makes it his honest endeavor to remove all stumbling blocks out of the beaten path.—[Chicago Inter-Ocean.

Send for Complete Descriptive List.

CHARLES P. SOMERBY, Publisher,

139 Eighth Street, New York.

PUBLICATIONS OF CHARLES P. SOMERBY.

Percy Bysshe Shelley as a Philosopher and Reformer. By CHAS. SOTHERAN. Including an Original Sonnet by C. W. Frederickson. Portrait of Shelley, and View of his Tomb. 60 pp., 8vo. Postpaid, paper, $1; cloth, $1.25.

> This is a paper read by its author before the New York Liberal Club. It is designed to take a philosophical view of Shelley's works, and present in regularly scientific form the philosophy which the poet taught, it may be almost unconsciously to h mself.—[St. Louis Globe-Democrat.

General Introduction to Social Science. [*Sociological Series, No.* **1.**] PART I. Introduction to Fourier's Theory of Social Organization. By ALBERT BRISBANE. PART II. Social Destinies. By CHAS. FOURIER. 8vo, clo., 272 pp. Postpaid, $1.

> The first of a series of Sociological works in which Fourier is taken up as the great Pioneer in the science. It contains both Mr. Brisbane's Introduction and Fourier's own Prospectus or outline sketch of his whole doctrine.

Theory of Social Organization. [*Sociological Series, No.* 2.] By CHARLES FOURIER. With an Introduction, by ALBERT BRISBANE. Cloth, 12mo, 612 pp. Postpaid, $1.50.

> This contains Fourier's Theory of Social Unity, and comprises essays upon the Social Destiny of Man, and a large variety of Sociological subjects. Mr. Brisbane claims that Fourier's theory is radically misunderstood by the general public, and that no true test of it has ever yet been made in practice. This and the preceding volume will do much toward furnishing a knowledge of the man and his teachings.

Essence of Christianity. By L. FEUERBACH. Translated by GEORGE ELIOT. Clo., gold side and back, 340 pp. Postpaid, $3.

Philosophy of Spiritualism, and the Pathology and Treatment of Mediomania. By F. R. MARVIN, M.D., Professor of Psychological Medicine and Medical Jurisprudence in the New York Free Medical College for Women. Clo. Postpaid, 75c.

> There is no way of getting rid of Infidelity till some way is devised of abolishing the doctors. And here is another point: he says the special indulgence in religious exercises undermines the fabric of morality.

Age of Reason, and Examination of the Prophecies. Being an Investigation of True and Fabulous Theology. By THOMAS PAINE, author of "The Rights of Man," "Crisis," "Common Sense," etc. With an Essay on his Character and Services, by G. J. HOLYOAKE. 12mo, 180 pp. Postpaid, pap., 50c.; clo., 60c.

Secularists' Manual of Songs and Ceremonies, for use at Marriages, Funerals, etc. Edited by AUSTIN HOLYOAKE and CHAS. WATTS. Flexible cloth, 12mo, 128 pp. Postpaid, 50 cents.

Herbert Spencer's First Principles. A Summary. By WM. A. LEONARD. Paper, 12mo, 48 pp. Postpaid, 50 cents.

The Christmas Festival: Its Origin, History and Customs. Together with a selection of Carols. By WM. A. LEONARD. Cloth, 12mo, 56 pp. Postpaid, 60 cents.

Music in the Western Church. A Lecture on the History of Psalmody, illustrated with examples of the Music of various periods. By WM. A. LEONARD, author of "The Christmas Festival," etc. Flexible cloth, 12mo, 89 pp. Postpaid, 75c.

Send for Complete Descriptive List.

CHARLES P. SOMERBY, Publisher,

139 Eighth Street, *New* York.

THE CHRIST OF PAUL;
Or, THE ENIGMAS OF CHRISTIANITY.

St. John never in Asia Minor. Irenæus the Author of the Fourth Gospel.
The Frauds of the Churchmen of the Second Century Exposed.

By GEORGE REBER.

12mo, Extra Cloth, 400 pp. Postpaid, $2.

CONTENTS.—Chapter I. Death of Stephen. Conversion of Paul. His retirement to Arabia, and return to Damascus and Jerusalem.

Chap. II. Paul and Barnabas start west to preach the Gospel. The prevailing ideas on religion in Asia Minor. Theology of Plato and Philo. The effect produced by the preaching of Paul. Chap. III. Therapeutæ of Philo, and Essenes of Josephus. An account of them. Their disappearance from history, and what became of them. Chap. IV. The origin of the Church. Chap. V. Review of the past. What follows in the future. Chap. VI. How the Four Gospels originated.

Chap. VII. John, the son of Zebedee, never in Asia Minor. John the Presbyter substituted. The work of Irenæus and Eusebius. John the Disciple has served to create an enigma in history. John of Ephesus a myth.

Chap. VIII. The Gnostics. Irenæus makes war on them. His mode of warfare. The Apostolic succession and the object. No church in Rome to the time of Adrian. Peter never in Rome, nor Paul in Britain, Gaul, or Spain. Forgeries of Irenæus.

Chap. IX. The claim of Irenæus, that Mark was the interpreter of Peter, and Luke the author of the third Gospel, considered. Luke and Mark both put to death with Paul in Rome. Chap. X. Acts of the Apostles. Schemes to exalt Peter at the expense of Paul. Chap. XI. Matthew the author of the only genuine Gospel. Rejected, because it did not contain the first two chapters of the present Greek version.

Chap. XII. The character of Irenæus, and probable time of his birth. His partiality for traditions. The claim of the Gnostics that Christ did not suffer, the origin of the fourth Gospel. Irenæus the writer. Chap. XIII. Why Irenæus wrote the fourth Gospel in the name of John. He shows that the Gospels could not be less than four, and proves the doctrine of the incarnation by the Old Testament and the Synoptics. The author of the Epistles attributed to St. John.

Chap. XIV. Four distinct eras in Christianity from Paul to the Council of Nice. The Epistles of Paul and the works of the Fathers changed to suit each era. The dishonesty of the times. Chap. XV. The Trinity, or fourth period of Christianity. Chap. XVI. The Catholic Epistles.

Chap. XVII. No Christians in Rome from A.D. 66 to A.D. 117. Chap. XVIII. The office of Bishop foreign to churches established by Paul, which were too poor and too few in number to support the Order. Third chapter of the second Epistle to Timothy, and the one to Titus, forgeries. The writings of the Fathers corrupted.

Chap. XIX. Linus never Bishop of Rome. Clement, third Bishop, and his successors to the time of Anicetus, myths. Chronology of Eusebius exposed; also that of Irenæus.

Chap. XX. The prophetic period. The fourteenth verse of the seventh chapter of Isaiah explained. Chap. XXI. Bethlehem the birthplace of Christ, as foretold by the prophets. Cyrus the deliverer and ruler referred to by Micah the prophet. The passage from the Lamentations of Jeremiah quoted by Matthew, chap. ii., verse 18, refers to the Jews, and not to the massacre of the infants by Herod.

Chap. XXII. Christ and John the Baptist. Chap. XXIII. The miracle of the Cloven Tongues. Misapplication of a prophecy of Joel.

Chap. XXIV. Miracles. Chap. XXV. Epistle of Paul to the Hebrews.

Chap. XXVI. The controversy between Ptolemæus and Irenæus as to the length of Christ's ministry. Christ was in Jerusalem but once after he began to preach, according to the first three Gospels, but three times according to John. If the statements made in the first three are true, everything stated in the fourth could only happen after the death of Christ.

Chap. XXVII. The phase assumed by Christianity in the fourth Gospel demanded a new class of miracles from those given in the first three. A labored effort in this Gospel to sink the humanity of Christ. His address to Mary. The temptation in the wilderness ignored, and the last supper between him and his disciples suppressed. Interview between Christ and the women and men of Samaria. A labored effort to connect Christ with Moses exposed.

Chap. XXVIII. The first two chapters of Matthew not in existence during the time of Paul and Apollos. A compromise was made between their followers at the Council of Smyrna, A.D. 107. The creed of the Church as it existed at that day determined, and how Christ was made manifest. Catholics of the second century repudiate this creed and abuse Paul. Further proof that Irenæus never saw Polycarp. Injuries inflicted upon the world by the fourth Gospel.

CHARLES P. SOMERBY, Publisher,
139 Eighth Street, New York.

ISSUES OF THE AGE;

OR,

CONSEQUENCES INVOLVED IN MODERN THOUGHT.

By HENRY C. PEDDER.

12mo, Extra Cloth, **Beveled**............Price, $1.50.

"The author of this volume has evidently kept company with many of the finer spirits of the age, until his mind has become imbued with the fragrance of their thought. He has excellent tendencies, elevated tastes, and sound aspirations."—*New York Tribune.*

"In the restless spirit of inquiry abroad, and the feverish excitement of doubt, he sees the returning glory of that intellectual empire which declined with Grecian culture. He has brought the fruits of a large culture and extensive reading, and a mind unusually calm and thoughtful, to bear upon the questions which are agitating the hour."—*N. Y. World.*

"An admirably written, scholarly volume."—*New York Daily Graphic.*

"**An** unprejudiced and thoughtful consideration of some of **the most** momentous questions that are now agitating the world, and will, no doubt, attract, as it deserves, the widest attention."—*N. Y. Commercial Advertiser.*

"The seven essays of this volume are all wise, candid, and free from harshness against conservatism, while they are in sympathy with liberal ideas. Mr. PEDDER is not one of those radicals who rail at the Christian religion. Indeed his rationalism has throughout a 'sweet reasonableness,' and is not the fierce dogmatism of those positive souls who would, with Voltairean directness, 'crush the infamous one.' We shall be glad to hear from him again."—*Christian Register*, (Boston).

"He presents a safe guide through the bewildering labyrinth of scientific, philosophical, and theological speculations, and evinces a thorough familiarity with most of the modern theories advanced."—*Jewish Times.*

"The author is evidently a man of genuine literary taste. His book exhibits reflection and independence."—*N. Y. Eve. Post.*

"A shining light in the peculiar school of philosophy which he affects."—*St. Louis Times.*

"A truly able discussion of the subjects which most vitally concern the higher nature and larger life of man."—*Chicago Evening Journal.*

"His views are characterized by a broad catholicity and a depth of thought which do credit at once to his heart and his mind."—*Grand Rapids Democrat.*

"Some of its chapters contain a power of analysis rarely surpassed. In many respects it is a valuable book for the student."—*St. Louis Dispatch.*

"A work of much more than ordinary interest. It contains profound and impressive thoughts and sentiments."—*Buffalo Post.*

"Its real merits can only be discovered by a perusal."—*Toledo Journal.*

CHARLES P. SOMERBY,

Publisher

Iron-Clad Series.

		Cents.
1.	The Atonement, by Chas. Bradlaugh	5
2.	Secular Responsibility, by George Jacob Holyoake	5
3.	Christianity and Materialism Contrasted, by Underwood	15
4.	Influence of Christianity on Civilization, by Underwood	25
5.	The Essence of Religion, by L. Feuerbach, paper	50
6.	Materialism, by Dr. L. Büchner	25
7.	Buddhist Nihilism, by Prof. Max Müller	10
8.	The Religion of Inhumanity, by Frederic Harrison	20
9.	Relation of Witchcraft to Religion, by A. C. Lyall	15
10.	Epidemic Delusions, by Dr. F. R. Marvin, paper	25
11.	The Masculine Cross and Ancient Sex Worship, paper	50
12.	The Principles of Secularism Illustrated. G. J. Holyoake	25
13.	Essay on Miracles, by David Hume	10
14.	The Land Question, by Chas. Bradlaugh	5
15.	Were Adam and Eve our First Parents, by C. Bradlaugh	5
16.	Why Do Men Starve? by Chas. Bradlaugh	5
17.	The Logic of Life, by George J. Holyoake	10
18.	A Plea for Atheism, by Chas. Bradlaugh	10
19.	Large or Small Families? by Austin Holyoake	5
20.	Superstition Displayed, with a Letter of Wm. Pitt, by Austin Holyoake	5
21.	Defense of Secular Principles, by Charles Watts, Secretary of the National Secular Society, London	5
22.	Is The Bible Reliable? by Charles Watts	5
23.	The Christian Deity, by Charles Watts	5
24.	Moral Value of the Bible, by Charles Watts	5
25.	Free Thought and Modern Progress, by Charles Watts	5
26.	Christianity: Its Nature, and Influence on Civilization, by Charles Watts	5
27.	Christian Scheme of Redemption, by Charles Watts	5
28.	Thought on Atheism, by Austin Holyoake	5
29.	Is there a Moral Governor of the Universe? A. Holyoake	5
30.	Philosophy of Secularism, by Charles Watts	5
31.	Has Man a Soul? by Charles Bradlaugh	5
32.	The Origin of Christianity, by Charles Watts	5
33.	Historical Value of the New Testament, by Chas. Watts	5
34.	On Miracles, by Charles Watts	5
35.	On Prophecies, by Charles Watts	5
36.	Practical Value of Christianity, by Charles Watts	5
37.	Progress of Christianity, by Charles Watts	5
38.	Is There a God? by Charles Bradlaugh	5

	Cents.
39.—Labor's Prayer, by Charles Bradlaugh	5
40.—Poverty: Its Cause and Cure, by M. G. H.	10
41.—The Value of Biography, by G. J. Holyoake	10
42.—Science and the Bible Antagonistic, by Charles Watts	10
43.—The Christian Scheme of Redemption, by Charles Watts	5
44.—The Logic of Death, by G. J. Holyoake	10
45.—The Character of Christ, by Charles Watts	5
46.—Atheism and the Gloucester Execution, by Chas. Watts	5
47.—Poverty: Its Effects on the People, by Chas. Bradlaugh	5

Other Iron-Clads are in active preparation.

The Manna Series.

	Cents.
1.—Original Manna for "God's chosen."	5
2.—B. F. Underwood's Prayer, per dozen	10
3.—New Life of David, by Chas. Bradlaugh	5
4.—Facetiæ for Free Thinkers	10
5.—200 Questions Without Answers	5
6.—A Dialogue Between a Christian Missionary and a Chinese Mandarin	10
7.—Queries Submitted to the Bench of Bishops by a Weak but Zealous Christian	10
8.—A Search After Heaven and Hell, by Austin Holyoake	5
9.—New Life of Jonah, by Chas. Bradlaugh	5
10.—A Few Words about the Devil, by Chas. Bradlaugh	5
11.—The New Life of Jacob, by Chas. Bradlaugh	5
12.—Daniel the Dreamer, by Austin Holyoake	10
13.—A Specimen of the Bible: Esther, by Austin Holyoake	10
14.—The Acts of the Apostles: A Farce, by Austin Holyoake	10
15.—Ludicrous Aspects of Christianity, by Austin Holyoake	10
16.—The Twelve Apostles, by Chas. Bradlaugh	5
17.—Who Was Jesus Christ? by Chas. Bradlaugh	5
18.—What Did Jesus Teach? by Chas. Bradlaugh	5
19.—New Life of Abraham, by Chas. Bradlaugh	5
20.—New Life of Moses, by Chas. Bradlaugh	5
21.—A Secular Prayer, by Austin Holyoake, per dozen	10

Other numbers of Manna for all sorts of hungry people are in preparation.

Send for Complete Descriptive List.

CHARLES P. SOMERBY, Publisher,
139 Eighth Street, New York.

www.ingramcontent.com/pod-product-compliance
Lightning Source LLC
Chambersburg PA
CBHW031606110426
42742CB00037B/1309